ONE WILD SONG

By the age of twenty-one, my son had sailed aboard a tall ship across the Atlantic and Pacific Oceans. At the age of twenty-two he wrote a poem which, once heard, can never be forgotten. At the age of twenty-three, he took his own life. This is what I did next . . . Cape Horn is renowned as one of the most remote and bleak parts of the world: the sailor's Everest. Paul Heiney set off from England — alone — to rediscover his son's voice through the medium of sailing, which Nicholas loved, and through the poignant poem that was his son's legacy. This is a story of adventurous seafaring, and of a man coming to terms with the greatest loss imaginable.

ONE WILD SONG

A voyage in a lost son's wake

PAUL HEINEY

ISIS
LARGE
PRINT

First published in Great Britain 2015
by
Bloomsbury Publishing Plc

First Isis Edition
published 2016
by arrangement with
Bloomsbury Publishing Plc

*A catalogue record for this book is available
from the British Library.*

ISBN 978–1–78541–294–3 (hb)
ISBN 978–1–78541–300–1 (pb)

Published by
F. A. Thorpe (Publishing)
Anstey, Leicestershire

Set by Words & Graphics Ltd.
Anstey, Leicestershire
Printed and bound in Great Britain by
T. J. International Ltd., Padstow, Cornwall

This book is printed on acid-free paper

"*I beg to remind the reader that the work is unavoidably of a rambling and very mixed character; that some parts may be wholly uninteresting to most readers, though, perhaps, not devoid of interest to all; and that its publication arises solely from a sense of duty.*"

ROBERT FITZROY, CAPTAIN, 1839, INTRODUCING HIS *VOYAGES OF THE ADVENTURE AND BEAGLE*

CONTENTS

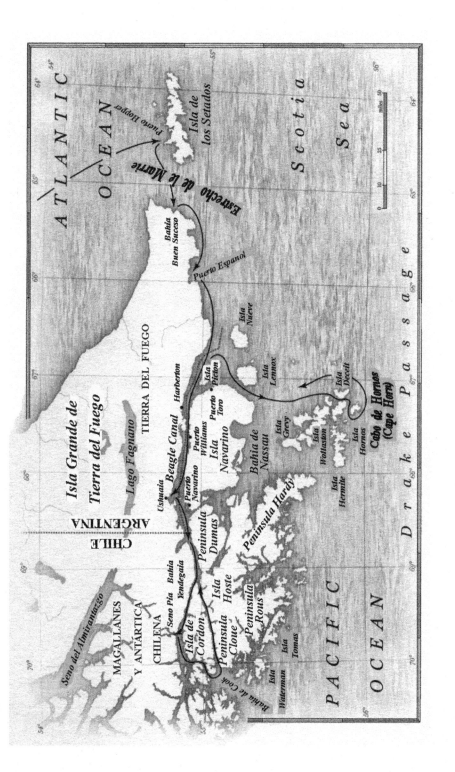

By the age of twenty-one, my son had sailed aboard a tall ship across the Atlantic and Pacific Oceans.

At the age of twenty-two he wrote a poem which, once heard, can never be forgotten.

At the age of twenty-three he took his own life.

This is what I did next.

INTRODUCTION

Land slips from sight very slowly, often more slowly than you would wish. But eventually it goes and in that moment, when the coast finally disappears and you, your little ship and your crew are alone on the sea, lies the torment; for a bit of you wants rid of the sight of land and the real journey to begin, but if you are honest you secretly crave its comforting presence. This is the voyaging paradox and has been for all sailors who take to deep waters. On that fine July afternoon, as the green and secure Cornish landscape dwindled behind me and the blank, grey ocean lay ahead, I was torn over where my true ambition lay: wouldn't life be simpler and safer at home, on land? Yet isn't an ocean voyage the greatest of achievements, if an often dangerous and uncertain business? Which way do you turn your head? Forwards to the unknown or backwards to the safe? The only answer has to be ever forwards, towards the bow. Backward glances are not the ingredients of true adventures.

The start of a new voyage is a time of confused emotions, a tumult of thoughts and feelings every bit as wild as the tumbling of the waves around you. This must be accepted and relished, for if depth of feeling is lacking then there can be no sense of adventure. On the one hand it is also a time of urgency in which you are drawn with all haste to the horizon like a gull to a scrap of fish: you want to be on your way, devouring the journey, making progress, putting miles beneath the keel, getting there. But a little bit of you wishes the land would stay with you, for it spells comfort and refuge while, increasingly, all around you is becoming less certain and you more isolated. On land you can walk with others, at sea you always stand alone.

It doesn't do to look over your shoulder too often, watching for the once distinct outline of land to fade to a blur and then be lost in the haze: this leads to an unnerving feeling that a door has finally closed on the world behind you. This thought will make you swallow hard. Yet once it is admitted, that things have changed and that which was is now gone, and only what lies ahead matters, then you are relieved and rise to the challenge. This transition does not always come easily, but it is at the heart of the satisfaction of voyaging. People talk of "voyages of discovery" and imagine only of arrivals in new, romantic worlds; but the beginnings and the ends in themselves are the least part of it, for true voyages are an unfolding process of self-discovery and the true drama lies not in the starting or the finishing, but is made along the way.

I have made two of my life's toughest voyages in the past few years: one I had always wanted to make, and the other I would have given anything to avoid. Both involved letting go of one world, and finding the courage to live in the next. One is the long trek, under sail, to one of the most profoundly remote parts of the world; to an often bleak land of rock, ice and near overwhelming storms — these are the waters of the infamous Cape Horn. The other is the long, hard journey through the death of my son, Nicholas, who took his own life at the age of twenty-three; to travel this road is to suffer desolation that no earthly place can inflict upon you. The two journeys are not unconnected; they are both tales of high adventure and discovery through some of life's most difficult landscapes, and both begin, as all voyages must, with finding the courage to face the future, reserving the past as a fond memory and not something you should cling to like a drowning soul. Your strength must come from what lies ahead. That is true voyaging.

Our first night at sea, the first after leaving England, had been kind to my wife, Libby, and me. Our boat, *Wild Song*, felt sure-footed as she made her way south in a following wind. She rolled and creaked in ways that were new to us, having owned her for only one full season, but already she was feeling like a friend. You need to be able to trust your boat for then, in return, she will grow into an extension of yourself, and already I felt a bond forming between us. By dawn we were abreast Ushant, the rocky, low island that is the far north-western fingertip of mainland Europe. Released now from home waters, spat out of the English Channel, we were now pointing our bows ever southward towards the Bay of Biscay, aiming for the island of Madeira a few hundred miles to the south-west of Portugal.

This was the first leg of a voyage to an uncertain place, in all senses, although it is true that already forming in my mind was the ultimate trophy, to sail around Cape Horn. There can be hardly a sailor who has not imagined what this place of grim reputation must be like, yet at the same time wanted to experience its wickedness for themselves. It is spoken of as an Everest. But how I might get there, and what I would do next if I ever achieved that, was far from decided.

From the moment when I first pulled out the charts to plot our course across the Bay of Biscay, I realised that without hardly any deviation we would pass close to an unmarked and unremarkable spot in the middle. It is defined only by imaginary lines of latitude and longitude, and is of no significance to anyone other than ourselves. It is 46.16N, 7.12W.

This was the spot where we scattered Nicholas's ashes a couple of months after his death. Did I mention that he'd taken his own life at the age of twenty-three? And did I also tell you that his sailing achievements at that young age eclipsed those of many voyagers who had lived far longer lives? He had sailed both the Atlantic Ocean and the Pacific under square sail aboard tall ships by the time of his twenty-first birthday. Not bad, my boy.

It is not for me to retell his adventures here, for in his writings published after his death he has told his own tale with more literary fluency than I could ever achieve. His work was edited by his mother and

Duncan Wu, his tutor at Oxford, and published under the title, *The Silence at the Song's End*. Nor shall I again describe the scene as Libby and I stood on the stern of the tall ship, *Europa*, scene of his greatest adventures, as she lay becalmed in the middle of Biscay on her journey from northern Spain to home waters. We were there to scatter his dusty remains. You will find my account of those moments, riven with tragedy and yet also with inspiration, within those pages also.

But I will tell you that I felt uneasy about revisiting the spot five years later. The last time we were there, to see his ashes descend into the unusually still waters of Biscay, the place had an unworldly feel to it. For all the sadness and bleakness of the moment, gleams of comfort shone through. I wondered if we would feel its force this time? We sailed slowly towards the spot. It was a late afternoon of typical Biscay weather — grey, choppy water under a leaden sky. I hoped and prayed that it would be special, like last time, because in that moment there was great closeness. But it seemed no different to anywhere else now. It was just the sea. I wanted another dose of the magic this place had held back then, but there was none. The GPS, the satellite-driven navigator which was leading us to the precise spot, had been displaying some unusual behaviour, which we dismissed with a laugh. Nicholas would have laughed too: "*You don't find me that easily.*"

We edged closer. I had stowed away a significant bottle of champagne, given to Nicholas by his headmaster for sheer pluck in refusing to accept anything other than Oxford University to study English, despite having been turned down at his first attempt only to triumph at the second. The bottle had never been opened. I could not bear the thought that the passing years would turn it sour. So as the GPS showed us to be within less than half a mile I brought it into the cockpit.

Being a bit muddled in the head by the emotion of the moment, I misjudged the drawing of the cork and the bottle popped a tenth of a mile from the intended spot. Libby and I had a good laugh. "I can hear him saying, 'Dad, don't bother. It doesn't matter.'" In fact, I could hear all three of us laughing out loud at the pointlessness of this gesture. In the end, that's what made the moment special. Within the laughter, within the imagined voice sharing the joke, there was great closeness. Libby and I toasted him with what turned out to be a poor example of wine-maker's art. We dashed the decks with the rank, fizzy wine and drank to the success of the voyage, wherever it might lead. With my last swig at the bottle I took what I vowed would be my last backward glance, intent on confronting a new frame of mind and facing a new future.

It is not unusual for sons to take their fathers as role models, for good or bad, but early on I decided that on this voyage it would be the reverse. From his writings I learned, for the first time if I am honest, of the true depth of his need for the sea and sailing. Many people sail in the wake of their heroes, and Nicholas would be mine. I was sailing to achieve the high standard that he had set, both in thoughts and deeds. That was my new-found ambition, crystallised in my mind at that moment. The sails drew us on, filled by a convenient northerly breeze which blew us ever south-westerly. We left his lonely way point behind and set our own course, just as he had chosen his. But we were not leaving him completely behind, for that would be to deny the past, without which there can be no future.

You might think it fanciful if I tell you that from that moment onwards I felt I had picked up a fellow traveller; but it is for me to know and you to mock if you wish. For that reason, during this long voyage to an uncertain place, you must expect to hear his voice as clearly as you hear mine. He will not be ever-present, he can offer no running commentary; he might come and go like the faintest of breezes, or not be heard at all. It is all beyond my control and understanding, but when thoughts of him emerge I must share them with you as honestly as I would if he were sitting at the wheel, flesh and blood again. He can no longer steer the ship, nor reef the sails, but his power to shape my thoughts and recollections remains.

And so, that understood, together we sailed onwards.

CHAPTER
ONE

THE VOYAGE BEGINS

The future is a forbidden place of which no glimpses are allowed, only guesses. Which was why, try as I might, I could not imagine what this voyage would be like. It would certainly take me to places I had never seen, to countries where I am a stranger, to parts of the ocean I have never sailed before in weather I might never have experienced. With the benefit of hindsight, I now realise that even an imagination at its most fertile could never have guessed at the inspiring sights that confronted my eyes, or the deepest feelings of both elation and dread that at times nearly overwhelmed me. Now, in flashbacks, I can see the deep electric blue of centuries past radiating as light from the crevasses of the Andean glaciers; I recall the wild green of ocean rollers advancing towards my little ship, foaming crests tumbling in wind that sings as sharp as a soprano. I can feel again the burn of a tropical sun, and the sweat of fear when walking through lonely, dark Brazilian docksides. I hear the rattle of the sails telling me something is amiss, and the cough of the engine that warns me it is about to die. I still feel a thrill at the memory of the dazzle of tropical night skies, and smile when remembering the friends I made along the way. But on that day, as we set off towards a dull, grey yonder, this was far in the forbidden future.

I started with only a vague plan, thankful that I am blessed a thousand times with a wife who supported not only this fuzzy notion but all the previous ones, notably my entry in the Azores and Back Race and then the Singlehanded Atlantic Race. My first, unconsidered thought, was to aim for the spot that so inspired Nicholas on his travels. After crossing the Pacific from north of Panama, and sailing for countless days beneath the spread of white canvas that propels the tall ship *Europa*, he arrived at Nomwin Atoll. You will not have heard of it; no one has. Google Earth shows it but only on maximum zoom. He memorably called it "the least lonely nowhere in the world". How could such a description render it anything but unmissable? I planned a little with that thought in mind but came to no serious conclusion for I have learnt that cruising plans are most often accomplished when never made in the first place. By all means have an idea in the back of your mind, a hazy sketch of how you might want things to turn out, but apply too much detail at too early a stage and you will be disappointed. It was when I found myself looking at the timetable of flights from Pohnpei, some 10,000 miles and several years of sailing away, that I decided it was getting ridiculous. I would plan one step at a time and see where that led me. After all, that was what Nicholas did. He set off on *Europa* with little precise idea where he would end up and found a whole world in which he never thought he would belong. Perhaps it is the free spirits who reap the greatest rewards.

Then came the issue of fitting out the boat. Different destinations call for differing approaches to the gear you should carry. It is as complex as packing for a holiday that takes you from the deserts to the poles; a craft destined for the tropics has requirements that would prove unnecessary in the land of the penguins. This was how I came to find myself, in the same week, discussing the installation of a near-atomic diesel heater and consulting on the kind of cockpit shade I should fit to deflect the equatorial sun. But some things are common to both regions. Your sails, rigging and engine must be sound, and so must your anchor. After that, all else is a bit of a luxury. Having said that, the list of luxuries can be quite-extensive. I bought a small machine, second hand, which (very slowly) converts seawater into fresh good enough for drinking. I changed the gas installation to propane instead of butane, which will not work in temperatures below zero. I had awnings made to catch the light tropical breezes which might drive some fresher and cooler air into the boat while at anchor. I invested in a sleeping bag deemed suitable for polar use, and bought mosquito nets to repel buzzing invaders. It was a schizophrenic kind of fitting out.

And, of course, it was never quite finished. I woke on the day of departure with a nagging sense that there was no washing-up liquid on board. On such details entire voyages can be won or lost.

The boat herself, *Wild Song*, I had few doubts about, yet although I thought I knew her pretty well, I didn't know her completely. I was more a stranger to this boat than to any we have had. I could not find a single thing. To feel that your boat is like a well-fitting glove is one of the most comforting sensations when you are at sea, but she pinched me like a pair of new-bought leather shoes. It would take a lot of effort before I could slide into her as easily as slipping into a pair of favourite loafers. Sooner or later we would have to fall in love, as all sailors do with their boats, but it hadn't happened yet. My relationship with her was a bit like marrying a woman on the basis of reviews written by others, and I was understandably nervous.

Those who have never sailed on a yacht before should know that it can be made to feel pretty much like home, if that's what you want. Some will prefer a spartan experience: sleeping in a damp bag, eating straight from a tin, washing up once a week, growing a beard to the knees. Not me. Although I was prepared to live like that if forced to by circumstances, a bit of home comfort gives me confidence — it is a smattering of order amongst the chaos. So, I slept most nights with a bright red duvet in a narrow but cosy berth towards the back of the boat from which I could see all the instruments showing the strength of the wind and the boat's speed, only needing to lift my head slightly from the pillow to get a full picture of what was going on. It was a short stride from there to the galley where, as long as the tanks were full, there was hot and cold running water and a gas cooker with four burners, grill and oven on which I could have catered for a wedding feast if required. From there it is just another short step to the saloon with its deeply upholstered green cushions around a large cabin table over which swings an oil lamp that casts a warm, yellow glow in the evenings. I had loudspeakers connected to a stereo system, but the locker which usually carried the booze was instead crammed with spares — so many of them that I lost track of where everything was. Right at the front, in the forepeak, are two wide and comfortable bunks for which I would have no use, so they served as stowage for a spare sail or two, several sacks of clothes to cope with all the climates of the world, and on occasion a sack of potatoes. It sounds as though I was setting sail in a rather comfortable bed and breakfast, but I knew the tossing of the sea would soon sort that out.

I'd had the reefing lines renewed with thinner but stronger line to reduce friction and make the effort of reducing the sails easier, but hadn't tested them. I panicked a little at the thought that something so important as being able to reduce the amount of sail you show to the wind should have been shoved on to the back burner. It was like being a mountaineer who had started his climb without a proper understanding of the knots that would hold his safety line.

I spent a day in Falmouth buying teabags, milk, onions, sticking plasters and rubber bands (to keep book pages open) until Libby arrived. She knew what to expect of her tetchy husband. He would be nervous, though trying not to show it; there would be tension in his speech, a brittle tone to his voice, a sharp word spoken when none was necessary. To let it all wash over her has been the burden of many a wife who has sent her husband off to sea. She reassures me without ever patronising me, restores me to my even keel when about to topple over, never tried to talk me out of this mad scheme, never quibbled over the cost, and, most generously of all, allowed me to take her half of the boat halfway across the world without her. It's one thing to part company with your husband, but another to be deprived of your boat.

We had an unpromising start. I was hooted at by the St Mawes ferry who didn't seem to think I was looking where I was going, which was true. And then I was waved at by a dive boat who thought I was too near to him, which was debatable. But worse was to come. We had refuelled and filled the diesel tank to the brim — a single fact that was to cast a shadow over the next few hours. Off a miserable headland called Black Head, just to the north-east of the Lizard, I went below and yelped. It was a cry of genuine hurt. There was a trickle of diesel running from the heater; an unstoppable river of vile, stinking oil flowing towards the bunk cushions without which there would be no comfort for many miles to come. There was so much of it that I guessed it had been dribbling ever since we caught the first gust and leaned over sharply. I was upset, dismayed and angry at this violation. It seemed such an insult, not only a despoliation of the whole boat, but surely a portent of poor fortune surrounding this project. I became angry out of all proportion. Libby, as so many

16

times before, saw a small problem in its true perspective. We sailed into shelter and quickly anchored off Coverack to clean up. It turned out that this was largely my own fault, for I had been advised on the installation by a man who understood only canal boats. They don't lean over. I never spotted that flaw in his instructions.

The afternoon faded and the events of the morning passed slowly from my over-anxious mind. I reached for the backstay and hauled myself to my feet and looked around. The sea was greyer as the sky grew darker, and rolling in a way that was neither inspiring nor memorable, just ordinary damned grey sea. But I remember thinking that, despite everything so far, I was glad to be there. Then a crash from below and my muscles tensed and imagination raced. A breakage? No, a can of peas had harmlessly fallen over. Time for the ever-calming kettle to be boiled once again.

In the dawn we slipped past the island of Ushant, the defiant western fingertip of northern Europe, which showed itself as a benign green island from which sprouted two lighthouses and a radar station. The first day was as good as sailing can be with the boat on an even keel (and me back on more of an even keel) and the galley work easy. I have always believed that things improve south of Ushant for then you are making real southing. I had no idea how I would feel when we finally came to the spot where Nicholas's ashes had been scattered, although, as I have already described, it did not feel special. Perhaps to expect it to be was a selfish notion. Darkness fell soon after and I took the first watch. If I am honest, I had hoped that I might hear his voice urging me on, wishing me luck, or more likely pulling my leg. But there was no whisper in my head. In the intense months after his death I will admit to having heard his voice, speaking to me, although his actual words I will keep to myself. Of course, you can dismiss this as the work of a distraught imagination, as I did in rational moments; but to feel something as powerfully as I did is completely different to imagining.

In almost any situation I can make myself imagine what he might say. If he were looking over my shoulder now and reading this, he would go, "Mmm, very interesting, Dad," and melt away. But that's imagination, not far short of guesswork. But when the words come as a distinct feeling they are different; they come out of the blue and are more powerful, cutting through everything like a searchlight through fog. I heard nothing that night, and was a little sad.

I felt at last able to open my mind and see far beyond the bow. I wanted, if not craved, some deeper satisfaction from this journey than from any sailing trip I had made before. I wanted the depth of experience that Nicholas had found, it was as simple as that. I decided that the maritime mantra of "keeping a sharp lookout at all times" did not confine itself to what was before my eyes. I must look all around me, and above too, at all that surrounds us, made that much more vivid by the isolation of a small boat on a big sea. The sea itself does not make this easy, not for me anyway because it is always master of my mood. I hate the sea when it rolls like a sheet of grey steel that has been flicked into motion — it is full of latent threat. The sea does not have to be rough to be nasty. One night I convinced myself we were sailing on mercury, so dull and metallic was the view. This made me low, and regretful that I had ever set out on this voyage. But I had a good sleep and felt better, well enough to curse a ship heading south on an almost parallel but slightly converging course. Would he pass ahead of me, or me ahead of him? I fretted, but Libby had a better method of dealing with such conflict. "I gave him a look," she said, "and he altered course."

I am not good at dawn watches. I have heard people romance about the joys of dawn at sea but I have always found it a cold and chilly experience made worse by the damp that has spent all night seeping through to your bones. Sunrise is another thing, and that is admittedly joyous, but you can keep the grey and dank first glimmers of dawn. However, this dawn was different for I decided I was becoming bored with myself and my general gloominess. We had just made a remarkable 140-miles-a-day passage in a fine little ship and we were both safe and well and there was nothing in the world that could cast any kind of shadow over me. Then I noticed the batteries were nearly flat. How boats do test you.

The seas were building in an irregular way and we were not entirely certain of how best to sail this new boat dead downwind in a rising gale. A couple of big waves rolled over the foredeck, green and heavy with our name on them, tumbling into the cockpit till we were submerged to the knees. The wind speed touched

30 knots, nearly a gale, and that was enough for us to alter course and run the 150 miles to the nearest harbour, at the mouth of the River Tagus, which leads to Lisbon. It turned into a wild ride but *Wild Song* made far lighter of it than we did. Compared with our previous sturdy old boats that sat in the water like hippos in a bath, this was supposed to be a modern flyer, but she showed every sign of being a mature sea boat despite her youthful age, and a fast one, for I think we cracked 162 miles that day.

It was early evening as we were escorted to a quiet berth in a marina of such vastness that a walk to the marbled halls of the marina office was not to be lightly undertaken. We had slipped, unknowingly, into the most expensive marina in western Europe.

I hoped for a better start to the trip than this.

CHAPTER
TWO

LEAVING HOME
WATERS BEHIND

I knew from the beginning that this trip was going to have to be done in chunks. I was still being invited to present a popular television series, *Countrywise* on ITV, and when you are approaching your mid-sixties and television executives still consider your ageing face can add some value to their ever more youthful channels, you do not turn down their invitation. It also pays for the trip. I considered them my sponsor.

A broken voyage has its drawbacks. A rhythm is established at sea which is best not fractured. But there are plusses, and they are to do with the seasonal way the winds blow around the oceans, at some times of year more cooperative than others. I needed the help of the north-east trade winds to get me south from Europe, then I wanted the breeze to be fair down the coast of Brazil and not against me. If I got as far as Patagonia, I wanted to be there in the summer when the days are long and comparatively warmer and where I would find the winds still fierce but the blows shorter. If I were to go further than the tip of South America, there were the great weather systems of the Pacific to consider. To expect all that to drop into place one after the other is asking a lot. In other words, I was not putting myself at a great disadvantage by breaking the trip and, more often than not, as it turned out, it worked to my advantage.

I returned to Portugal, alone, at the beginning of September. I saw that the Portuguese trade winds were blowing strongly from the north which was good news as it meant a fair wind south. Nothing seemed as important as getting on with the voyage. I felt as if I had experienced the first strike of the match against the box but yet there were no flames. I was ready for this project to ignite.

I was driven from the airport by a young Portuguese taxi driver who was unashamedly enthused by the idea of going to sea, as I suppose a young man with such rich, salty blood in his Portuguese veins should be. All the places I was aiming for, he pointed out with bursting pride, were discovered by the great Portuguese navigators. Then, to my astonishment and a certain shame at my own ignorance, he recited his way around the Atlantic rim ticking off the names of his heroes who had sailed there: Vasco da Gama, Magellan, and Henry the Navigator who started it all with his navigational academy, which was to inspire the Portuguese to conquer the unknown world, and still caused this lad's pulse to race.

It is easy to be inspired by the sea, but harder to cope with the more mundane demands that sea-going makes. Although I loved being back on the boat and was fired up to be on my way again, I was niggled to find the batteries had gone flat once more. Without batteries there is no electricity to drive the navigation instruments or the windlass for lifting the anchor, and in the very worst case no power to start the engine. To this could be added already failed navigation lights, and unreliable instruments that for some reason repeatedly blew fuses. I should have moved all those things higher up the priority list but it was too damned hot. I was taken aback to be stopped by a young couple who were setting off on their first Atlantic adventure and saw me as a source of wisdom on such matters. I have always felt I am a beginner at this game. I told them they would be fine. What else was there to say? I hope they made it, that young couple: he fresh out of the army with his focus on "outcomes" and "objectives", she asking how rough it would be.

For the leg to the Canary Islands, a passage of 400 miles, I took on two crew who arrived just in time to miss the lugging of the heaviest stores. Ant and Chris, both of whom have sailed with me before, are as agreeable a couple of hands as you could wish for. Chris, a decade older than me, has an analytical mind that works like no other I have come across. He can extract from the simplest of tasks a heap of conundrums that would never occur to me, and allow himself no rest until his mind has fully thought through every aspect that is weighing on it, even if the result might have no practical relevance — it is the intellectual journey that matters. It must be very tiring. I asked him to consider the arrangement of the many blocks and pulleys that make up the mainsheet with which you trim the boom and thereby the mainsail. Was it too complicated? I asked. Could it be improved? He sketched away for a while before going silent on the matter. Then, later that night, when I woke him at 2am to stand his watch, his eyes snapped open and he blurted, "You can do without blocks 4 and 5!" You could see from the look on his face that the struggle of arriving at that conclusion, played out through his slumbering hours, had brought him great satisfaction. The only problem I was totally unable to solve, and for which he could give me no help, was why he had bought so many green beans when doing the final shop before departure. I well understand that the capacity to delegate can be a great attribute in a skipper, but when it comes to the matter of the galley I am reluctant to let go, as in my experience this is the sort of thing that happens. I had green beans bursting from every food net and locker and all destined, I reckoned, to go rotten long before they could be cooked. If we'd eaten them for every meal we could not have saved all of them from putrefaction. It wasn't as if any of us was particularly enamoured with beans. And all this from an individual who came across as a man who knew how many beans made five.

Ant, who loves nothing better than to be at sea, is always a source of good humour on a boat. He may not take the academic approach to life that Chris prefers, but a man who can quickly grab for a spanner and save the day can sometimes be more useful than one who debates long and hard the best tool for the job. They made for a nicely balanced pair. Early on, Ant galvanised us with the news that he had constipation. Conveniently, I prescribed green beans in large quantity, but his brave consumption of them hardly made a dent in the supply, nor moved his bowel much.

We sailed south towards Morocco and I sensed that ahead lay places radically new to me. Off Casablanca I noticed that this bit of sea felt somehow "different", although I couldn't explain how. It is remarkable how spots on the open ocean can have a character and atmosphere of their own, but remain the same sea. There are places you feel at home, others where you are less sure of yourself, and some that are downright creepy. All the same sea, though.

The colour of the water was slowly changing to a powder blue when the sun shone, and the wind remained gently on the port quarter, which makes for the easiest point of sailing, so no apprehension here. With the wind blowing gently off the land I expected at least a sniff of north Africa, but nothing came. Bird life was sparse, marine life too, and when I excitedly told Chris that I had seen a very fat dragonfly whizz past, he thought for a while — never rushing to judgement — before deciding it couldn't have been. More likely a distant flying fish, he thought. Still, that was something.

We rolled like drunks over the Atlantic swells that built ever higher as the sea closed the shore. And then, as if a switch had been thrown, the rise and fall ceased as we came into the shelter of low rocks extending from a golden, sandy shore, and we found ourselves in the small Moroccan port of Essaouira, a bustling, stinking harbour where workmanlike trawlers lay thick alongside the quay, and where black faces of all ages scurried to and fro with arms full of fish. There was fish on the boats, fish in the gutters, fish on the pavements. More fish than in the sea. This was, unmistakably, the African continent and chaos reigned. A couple of hundred miles from Lisbon felt like a thousand.

To arrive in your own boat in an unknown harbour on an unknown coast is an experience more potent than any other form of travel can provide. You have changed elements from earth to sea and back again, and harnessed the natural forces of the weather to achieve your transport, and for that reason the thrill of arrival is all the more. It is a simply a greater kind of victory.

No smart yachting facilities here, no, sir. This was a working harbour and we had to fit in as best we could. With a flurry of animated waving and shouting from the shore we were directed alongside a rusting, red hulk of a boat that seemed of little use to anybody. It turned out to be the lifeboat. We offered the cheerful and helpful skipper a beer for his trouble, after hastily asking if, in a country where the Muslim religion held sway (if lightly), this might be a problem for him. "If it is a small one, the Prophet says it is OK," he replied, with a grin. I liked this place. Elderly women gutted fish on the quayside; sharks were landed and quickly carved into chunks. Children swarmed like worker ants round the fishermen who were landing swordfish from bright blue open fishing boats and butchering their catch by the roadside to let the blood flow back into the sea. Around the wooden frames of old fishing boats that were either being restored or demolished — it was difficult to tell the difference — feral kittens played while dogs sat and scratched themselves. Everything in this harbour was constantly in motion. Nothing paused for breath. It seethed.

It was time to make our arrival official. Our first visit was to a small building of faded colonial aspect a little way back from the harbour, looking as though it had been left there by the makers of the *Casablanca* movie. We climbed two stone steps, accidentally disturbing the blind cat that stood guard. Behind the shutters sat the uniformed immigration officer with a pistol on his hips and the required severe look on his face. His desk was bare apart from a notepad. On the wall were "WANTED" posters with threatening pictures of evil desperadoes sought for all crimes including murder. For technology, an old Imperial manual typewriter sufficed.

The officer moved slowly to copy all our passport details, stroking his moustache between every word he wrote, and with a pencil he scribbled painfully slowly on his pad in his best joined-up writing. This took him the best part of half an hour, after which he went to the next room and copied out everything on to a clackety computer so elderly it must have pre-dated Bill Gates. Then came the sound that over the course of the voyage was to become the finest I could hear, as satisfying as a chorus of angels. It is the final and definitive *thump-click* of the rubber stamp on the official papers. It is only when you hear it in all its glorious crescendo that you know for sure that your problems are over, at least for the moment.

With regret, we sailed away around mid-morning the next day and faced a glassy ocean. Light wind sailing can be concentrated work, and paradoxically can be as damaging to a boat and its rigging as a gale of wind. As the boat rolls to the swell, which is always found at sea even on the calmest days, the sails slat backwards and forwards, coming up hard against the ends of the ropes that hold them. It is this constant movement followed by sudden arrest which, over the hours, does the damage. A sail that does not properly fill with wind is a sad and pathetic sight; all its potential is wasted as it becomes as useless as a flat party balloon. You would think that to sail dead downwind with the breeze directly behind you would be the easiest thing in the world to do, but it requires far more attention than any other point of sailing and becomes all the more tiring when you are making little progress. We rigged lines to hold the boom in position, employed a "boom brake", which helps to prevent its sideways crashing, then rigged a pole from the mast to hold out the yankee, which is our largest headsail and is brightly coloured. We must have looked like a floating circus tent by the time the whole lot was rigged. It was one more step in the learning process that makes your boat a seamless extension of yourself. There are no shortcuts to achieving it. You simply have to put in the miles, even if they are slow ones.

Eventually the wind filled in and we sped to Lanzarote. The sea came alive with a whale which the others claimed to have seen but I did not, and then a school of dolphins diving and cavorting alongside us, crisscrossing the bows so close that collision looked inevitable, but they always won clear. A game developed, dolphin versus boat, to see who had the best underwater profile for sliding through the water. Nature seemed to have the edge. The cockpit sunshade made its debut as the midday sun grew stronger, and on a largely flat sea meals were eaten from the cockpit table as easily as if we were on land. The crew had obeyed my express orders and each had brought from home a couple of hundred tea bags to satisfy an innate need in all voyagers (certainly this one) for a constant supply of stimulating tea. While sailing with a friend, he remarked that I took so much of the stuff that it was "like having the builders in". Nevertheless, when taken with those flaky, little custard tarts with their cinnamon, lemon and vanilla so beloved by the Portuguese, serenity was the order of the day.

Chris woke me in the night to say the batteries were flat and low voltage alarms were bleeping at him from various instruments, which was depressing. There was plenty to nag the mind, yet as I write this in hindsight such worries seem trivial. But to dismiss them as such at the time is to fail to understand the magnification that takes place on a small boat in the middle of the ocean. Far from being free, your world is now confining. What is within the length of the boat is all you have, and if a battery becomes flat then that is a large proportion of what matters to you and your survival in this restricting bubble in which you now live.

The greatest nag of all, though, was the 3,500 miles to Salvador in Brazil. These miles I intended to sail alone. That in itself is no big deal by the standard of modern sailing, and I can't explain why it worried me so much, for this is one of the ocean passages of the world where the weather can generally be reckoned as safe with the winds and currents favourable. Its outcome should be as certain as a helter-skelter ride. Nor should the distance worry me. I had spent 35 days alone at sea when I competed in the 2005 singlehanded transatlantic race and this leg of the passage should take far less than that. My worry was that I simply didn't know the place as I did the English Channel, or the north Atlantic, or any of the other places I had sailed. But looking at it sensibly, no stretch of water stays the same for long, and any particular place that is remembered for its placidity can turn within minutes into a dreaded spot where life can hang by a thread. So perhaps you can never feel completely at home on the ocean, for to be "at home" implies a sense of comfort through stability, which the sea never allows you.

By dawn on the third day we were almost upon Lanzarote. Ant set to work with the frying pan, slapping the bacon into it and sending through the boat that most stimulating salty scent of all.

In sharp contrast to the fish-strewn quaysides of Morocco we entered a swept and manicured concrete development, Puerto Callero, where both the bollards and manhole covers were made of bronze. What a waste. Why didn't they spend the money instead on replacing the cheap metal cleats that held the boats secure? This island may be big on sunshine and hotels, but when it comes to allure it is sadly lacking. Like all volcanic islands — and I was to stumble across many of them — the abiding question is why anybody bothers to cling to these dusty, arid outcrops at all. And why does anyone come here for a holiday? You might as well take a break on an ash tip. This must be a marvellous place for a geography field trip. But not much else. You really do have to get a thrill from the sight of lava to get anything out of Lanzarote.

Ant and Chris set about planning their flights home but I could focus on nothing but the next leg. We spent a nervous hour drinking coffee with little said, none of us wanting to talk of what might lie in store for me once I was sailing alone. My tension was relieved when, after saying, our goodbyes, I came across a supermarket where I was able to secure both vacuum-packed bacon and tinned butter, which were to prove invaluable. But I was less lucky when it came to hunting down a man to stamp my passport to give me final clearance from our great European Union. No one was bothered, no one was available, no one cared. The passport office in the docks area was empty. Only a lone security guard suggested, "You might come back on Thursday. There's sometimes somebody here. But not always." It was Monday and I wasn't waiting. The last exit stamp in my passport was on leaving Morocco. When I got to the next foreign country I would have to lie and tell them I had sailed directly from there.

I left Europe already feeling like a man on the run.

CHAPTER
THREE

"I SING INSIDE MYSELF"

I have sailed many thousands of miles in my life, but for very few of them have I ever given serious thought to what it really means to cross oceans, why we are driven to it, what effect it might have on our selves. My life has been immeasurably enhanced by the part that the sea has played in it. Perhaps now was the time to discover why.

That's what Nicholas achieved in his short lifetime — a deep understanding of the sea. I craved the lucidity of his insights. His reflections and introspections gathered in a mere five years eclipsed a thousand-fold any paltry thoughts I might have captured in over forty years. I wondered if I might find an emotional fluency that had been largely lacking for most of my life, one which might not make a comfortable cruising companion? I've never thought any feelings I might have mattered much to anyone else, but I now see that it is only by sharing them that we enable others to compare and understand their own. We should all open up more. Not in a "look at me" way, but more as a pointer so that other people can look fresh at themselves.

At the forefront of my mind was a poem written by him. I have never been a great reader of verse due to the abusive kind of English teaching I was subjected to at a 1960s northern grammar school. Perhaps it wasn't their fault; it may have been mine for having a mind unwilling or unable to make the leap of imagination that transforms blank words on a page into elevated visions of beauty or insight. I look at poetry with a too clinical eye, always wanting to know what the writer is getting at, and when I don't see it straight away I cast the verse aside with a curse — why can't these bloody people just come out with it and say what they mean?

I know it is a huge gap in my life, and I have always been ready to open my heart to what poetry has to offer, but I have found few verses with which I could forge a relationship. Too many poems have left me with a feeling of frustration at my own failure of understanding, and for that reason poetry is not something to which I would ever turn for either comfort or inspiration. If there is a poetic blindness which, like colour blindness, makes all things grey, then that is what I have.

I can never be confident I've got hold of the right end of the stick. I know that rhythm is part of the poet's game but, apart from the dum-di-dum of popular verse, I often can't see it. I have a deep suspicion that some poets rather like it that way; it keeps the intellectual riff-raff, like me, out of their worlds. There again, it is possible that much poetry which presents itself as difficult is not problematical at all; it is simply rubbish. But those who can say that with confidence

33

have the eyes and ears to sense it. I do not. I've been told I should relax more, allow a "washing-over-me" kind of process to take place, and see what emerges. But I am too technical of mind, and want clearly defined answers to the abiding question — what the hell is this all about? This wouldn't normally matter. It is quite easy, and not unfulfilling, to live a life with no poetry in it, and still to have a sense of the "poetic".

But this must change. Now was the time to make the effort, and this voyage would provide the mental space. It would only be through reading Nicholas's poems that I might gain a fuller understanding of him, and to achieve that would be worth all the effort I could summon, and more. His poetry unlocks the door into his world, and although I have not been given the eyes to even see the key, let alone deploy it, that does not mean I cannot continue the search. It is now all I have of him — his words.

There is one poem in particular. It was the one that gave the title to his book, and I have presumed to steal a few words from it to give the title to my own. It was amongst the last he wrote.

I can never know if he saw the end of his own life coming — for what it's worth I believe he did — but talk of "song's end" might mean just that. Or not. Here it is, in full:

The morning runs
on, a springtime secret
through the avenues

and avenues which lure
all sound away

I sing, as I was taught
inside myself.
I sing inside myself
when wild moments
slice some tender evening
like a breeze
that rattles gravel
and digs in the dirt

I sing, as I was told,
inside myself.
I sing inside myself
the one wild song, song that whirls
my words around
until a world unfurls

my ship's new sail
I catch the dew and set
a course amongst the ocean curls
The silence at the song's end
Before the next
Is the world.

What do you think? No, I'm not certain either, but there are many miles ahead in which to try to fathom it, so let's not rush it. Take it step by step, little by little. So far I have lazed in my bunk and read it in my head; I have stood by the wheel and read it loud hoping that there might be a revelation in its rhythm and metre. It has not yet come to me, although I have a sense of the musicality of it. I hear the timid swirling of the breeze in my head as I read it. Perhaps that is progress.

I made sure that poem was everywhere around me. It is in the name of my boat, *Wild Song*; those words are engraved in brass and screwed to the bulkhead so that every time I sit down the words are before me. It is all around me and forever will be. So few words, yet so important.

It became like a Rubik's cube in the pocket of my sailing jacket; something to play with, to twiddle, till everything dropped into place. It was his great gift to me as I sailed on. Part of him, with me, heading for distant places, together seeking understanding.

CHAPTER
FOUR

ALONE AT LAST

There is no worse feeling than emerging from a harbour mouth feeling like a happy rat going a'hunting, only to find threatening grey rollers coming at you like runaway trains. The first one hits, makes its relentless way from the bow swirling aft along the deck, before cheekily spurting through the one hatch you have left open, soaking your pillow, from which the salt water will never dry. Then the boat leans away from the gusting wind like a boxer who has caught an unexpected blow. Cups and pans crash as if an earthquake has rumbled through. How you wish you were back in the harbour.

But not on this morning. I motored towards the southern tip of Lanzarote, knowing it was time for my singlehanding instincts to take charge and the old habits of self-sufficiency to kick in. *Wild Song* had renewed vigour too, as if she was ready and eager to be on her way. It was teamwork now.

It is a rewarding feeling to be completely at home on a boat and that morning I felt comfortable with her, a stronger sense of comradeship than at any time before. In fact, so uplifting was the feeling of being back at sea that the dismal island of Lanzarote seemed to display rather more character than I had seen up till now and looked almost intriguing, her bleakness diminished. Perhaps there is something about places seen from the sea. Is it a kind of perfecting prism? Or perhaps to see the world from seaward is always to observe a better place. Anyway, it looked pretty good.

I paid the price for my relaxed frame of mind. Just as dawn was breaking the next day I realised that I had been foolish not to have taken action earlier: our course was bringing us desperately close to the island of Grand Canaria. It is one thing to see street lights on the shore, but when you can seen people on bikes and almost read the headlines on their newspapers, you are probably a little too close. The wind was freshening now, as it tends to when it funnels between these high islands, accelerating over the volcanic peaks and inching me ever closer to the rocks.

I made a muddled decision to set a sail with which I had little experience, a strange cocktail of a sail that at first glance is billowing and colourful like a light, floaty spinnaker — a large balloon-like sail that flies from the masthead and catches the wind when it is blowing from behind. But on closer examination the so-called Parasailor betrays its heritage, for it comes out of the parachute and not the sailmaking world. It claims that most beguiling of characteristics — easier handling. Now, in a freshening wind, closing the shore, and early in the day when my senses were dull, I decided I would hoist it for the first time, alone.

The rigging of the lines, which are four in total, took some time as each involved a trip to the foredeck and back, and then the tedious threading of all four lines through four blocks, or pulleys. It is very easy to get into a tangle, which then requires more journeys forward, over which I was taking excessive care since the first rule of singlehanding is to stay aboard the boat. When all that is done, the sail can be hoisted in a kind of long, thin nylon sock, like a sausage skin, which can be unpeeled when you are ready.

With heart thumping, I raised the sock. The sail billowed in the wind, cracking in the fresh breeze, the sheets flying like writhing snakes possessed of demons. I sprinted back to the cockpit, threw the lines round winches and attempted to gain control, which eventually came. Or not quite, for something looked wrong. I had hoisted the sail inside out. I had screwed up.

Back to the foredeck, praying with every step that when I tugged on the line that would douse the sail, it would happen as requested. It did. I reversed the sheets, thinking I had reversed the sail, and hoisted it again. This time it was twisted, and when I tried to douse it, it would not budge. So back to the cockpit to ease sheets, mind racing as to what I would do if the damn thing was stuck. I noticed the wind speed was now 20 knots, which I have since decided is the sort of figure at which you start thinking of bringing this sail in and not setting it.

I remember the greatest sense of relief when it was finally back in its bag, tamed, quelled and lashed to the deck from where it could not rise up like a malevolent monster and give me further trouble. I was totally exhausted, not entirely by the physical effort but more subdued by the realisation that complete familiarity with all the workings of this boat was still some way off. I re-rigged a more comfortable headsail and we proceeded on our way under full control and in comfort, as we should have done in the first place. As I said, there is a limit to the value of enthusiasm on a boat. Time spent in consideration can be more productive. Anyway, I could now steer a course clear of the land and contemplate breakfast.

Every day brought some kind of hiatus even though the wind was fair and moderate with the sea rolling along with only an easy and unthreatening swell. For example, later that day, when still in the shadow of the islands and affected by the disturbed winds that funnel through them and skirt around them, the wind got on the wrong side of the sails and the boat gave a violent lurch to port, scooping up several bucketfuls of water across the deck as she did so. This scurried down the side deck and in through the galley window, cascading on to the stove and soaking the teabag jar, which I had left without its lid. In my small world, this was a huge catastrophe. The incident was made worse by Libby's constant yet often ignored reminder to "close the lids", which now resonated in my head.

As I sorted the tangle of sails, I became aware that I had a tendency to spend far too much time sitting in the cockpit hoping problems would go away rather than trying to solve them. To be forced into action was good for me. It may be all part of the process of understanding the ways of the sea and boats, and trying to see both of them as ally rather than sometime enemy. There again, I wonder if you can ever call the sea your friend? I have never heard a real mariner speak of it that way. Part of the thrill seems to be that you can never be certain from minute to minute whether it is on your side or against you. It was getting dark. I opened an exotic food tin, bought at a French market by my daughter and gifted to the boat — a hearty feast of sausages and lentils. Quite perfect for the moment.

There are certain "management" issues that have to be confronted when it comes to getting a small boat across an ocean, and these began to occupy my thoughts. For a start, I became gripped by a sense that things were not happening at quite the right time. I had got myself out of tune with the rising and setting of the sun. Ships under way must adjust their clocks, one hour for every fifteen degrees east or west, or you end up in the situation in which I was finding myself with dawn getting later and later, so that when the clock read 8am, daylight was only just breaking, and sunset was well past nine o'clock. The solution is to put the clock back an hour, which I did, but I found it very unsettling. In only three days I had developed domestic habits, such as listening to the BBC World Service while having breakfast, enjoying the news digest followed by a snappy arts programme — a perfect accompaniment to toast and tea. But now I would have to eat an hour earlier if I was to keep up with their schedule, which runs to GMT; likewise my end-of-the-day listening habits were also thrown and it took me a good 48 hours to adjust to new ways. I decided I would adjust the clock to suit me. As long I could know the precise time according to GMT, what did it matter? So, we were now on WST — *Wild Song* Time — all the way to Brazil. I had no intention of endlessly fiddling with the hands of the clock like some nervous Swiss cuckoo-clock maker.

Then comes the issue of electricity, and having enough of it. This is an ever-present problem on an ocean-cruising yacht. Of course, you can transport yourself back to basics and have none at all: Vasco de Gama managed without an iPad. But there's no halfway house with electricity: once you've got one thing that needs it then you gather others until it suddenly dawns on you that you need not only a small power station to run them all, but an energy strategy to keep them going. Taken together with the complexity and vulnerability of a lot of modern devices in a marine environment, the whole business of keeping the kit going can turn into a major headache for ocean voyagers. You only have to read the accounts of racing sailors who are pushing their boats to the limits to discover that it is often the electrics that fail before anything else. I was already aware that my batteries were not in the best condition so, in a sense, I was already compromised. But I didn't feel it. I had a good compass and a mechanical device called a Walker log which I could trail through the water to tell me how far I had travelled. If you know which way you are going and how far you have gone then you have a reasonable idea of where you are — it's that simple. For added accuracy there are always the stars, sun and planets to observe, although that requires a little more application, as I was soon to discover.

Then comes the all-important business of getting rest. Sleeping while singlehanded sailing is the thing I am most asked about. "What do you do for sleep?" people will ask. Some even say, "Do you go into a harbour every night?" And that is when I have to contain my impatience. Would they ask an Everest climber if they found nice B&Bs on the way up? So many people know so little of what it is like to be at sea. Let me give you the proper answer: you should sleep for fifteen to twenty minutes at a time, no longer. According to research, this will provide you with sufficient sleep yet at the same time enough awareness of events around you. I had a kitchen timer to keep me disciplined. So the routine is: drop off to sleep having set the timer. Brring! You awake with a curse and stick your head out. Ninety-nine times out of a hundred there is nothing to be seen and nothing to do. Reset the timer. Back to sleep for another 20 minutes. And on it goes through the night. It may sound disruptive, but your disconnection is brief to the point of hardly being disconnected from sleep at all. There's also another good reason for the short-nap method of sailing. Your only real enemies are other vessels — big ships (assuming you are far enough offshore to avoid fishing fleets). It is a reasonable bet that if you go to sleep with a clear horizon, by the time you next look round fifteen minutes later, any ship that was invisible to you a quarter of an hour before will not be close enough to be a threat. So goes the theory, and undoubtedly it's the best practice.

Now to the real world of ocean slumbering. If you read the voyaging accounts of the early singlehanders such as Francis Chichester and Alec Rose, it quickly becomes clear that on many occasions, when weather allowed, they would have a damned good supper about nine o'clock at night, turn in, and if a change in the weather did not disturb them then they would be up just in time for a proper breakfast the next morning. This at a time when ships on the high seas were smaller and so there were more of them. Of course, a change in the weather is the best alarm of all, for it would be a poor sailor who didn't wake instantly there was a change in the motion of the boat. It takes very little — the mere flap of a sail will do it — to have you sitting bolt upright, rocketed out of deep sleep, sensing that something is not quite right. There is more to it than this, though, for many solo sailors have reported waking for no apparent reason, yet when they look out there is an approaching ship on the horizon. Dogs, they say, can sense when their owner is walking down the street although they can't see or hear them. Might we have a similar instinct that has become submerged by the general noise of life, and might the peace and solitude of the ocean be the last place we sense it?

The open seas are deserted places. Even when you are a handful of miles from land you might as well be a thousand. The horizon is unbroken all around, and ships become a rare sight. When I sailed the north

Atlantic alone over a distance of 3,500 miles, I saw only four other ships the whole way and none of them was a threat to me. So you do a balancing act in your mind, trying to rationalise your need for a good, long sleep (in itself a safety procedure), while avoiding the risk of being run down because you didn't see the other man coming. There are no rules to getting it right that I can figure out, and no guarantees either. You have to get a feeling for the right thing to do and stick with it. Instincts must sometimes guide actions. Some nights I slept a good six hours at a time; others I might have been up and down every half hour, but I couldn't explain why.

Five days out and the speed was dropping. Four knots I am happy with, but when those infuriating digital numbers flicker around the 2.5 mark then I start to get uneasy, more so when it is late in the afternoon as I am not too keen on major sail changes in the dark unless absolutely necessary. It's strange, and ridiculous, how the difference of a mere knot of boat speed can turn you from the most fretful to the happiest bloke on the high seas.

Pleasure only lasts so long at sea, otherwise everyone would be out there doing it, I suppose. If ocean sailing was one long party we'd all be at it. Since the wind was dropping now, I decided it was time to take action. Rather than gobble up diesel to make electricity, I hung a small, water-driven generator from the stern, powered by a two-bladed turbine, like a propeller, which trailed 30 yards behind the boat; the spinning of the turbine as it was pulled through the water forced the generator to spin, giving me a useful few amps. The only drawback was that it made an irritating noise, like a snoring dog. It is strange how an annoyance can quickly turn into company. I missed it when it stopped.

The drawback is that it slows you down a little and we were already wallowing. It was time to haul in the line. I got out a plastic funnel I had modified by slitting it lengthways so it could be opened up; I wrapped the funnel round the line, secured it, and hoped it would not come open. The idea was that this would run down the line and eventually stop the flow of water over the turbine, making the line easier to pull in. I was wrong. Halfway through its travel towards the distant end, the funnel escaped. The only way to retrieve the line now was to pull it in. It would be like trying to land a fighting shark.

I reached for a pair of sailing gloves and put them on. Then I started to haul on the line. The hauling itself is tough, but not impossible, though the whole process is rendered more difficult by the spinning of the rotor, which does not stop as long as the boat is making some forward motion. Soon the line kinks into ever tighter loops till you no longer have a single line but a mass of tightly twisted rope. The more you pull, the worse it gets. And then, painfully, the tip of one of my gloves, the index finger I think, caught in the middle of some kinks, which then wrapped themselves tightly round my finger with the speed and grip of a python. My arm was being drawn by the line to which I was fatally attached, and I risked being dragged over the stern of the boat.

Had there been a sudden gust of wind causing the boat to accelerate, this would certainly have happened.

The tightening was now beginning to hurt. I contemplated the loss of a finger, but I could wriggle it, just, inside the glove, and I struggled like Houdini himself, finally pulling my hand free. The glove remained, trapped and spinning as a reminder of a close call. But the problem of retrieving the line was still not solved, and it was only with a mighty exertion that I managed to get the line as far forward as one of the big winches and could then wind it in, kinking itself as it came aboard like something demented, until all 30 metres of it landed in the cockpit as tight as a ball of solid rubber. My arms ached with a deep pain, my body as wet with sweat as a drowned dog.

At sea, you must take your pleasures when you can, for sure enough something will be along soon to spoil your entire day.

CHAPTER
FIVE

FOLLOWING THE STARS

I sailed through darkness yet the darkness itself shone out night after glorious night. I was just 20 degrees north of the equator now, and loving the darkest night as much as the brightest day.

I am no stranger to the dazzle of the Milky Way but I had never seen it quite like this before. It flashed like the biggest ever spark across the sky, as vivid as a white road-marking applied with a broad brush. There was no divide between inky sea and black sky. It was all enveloping. The stars no longer revolved around the world: they turned around me. To be alone on the ocean is to be close to the heart of everything.

Everyone should practise the art of astro-navigation, the method by which you can find your position on the face of the earth by observation of the heavenly bodies. It gives you a direct connection to things beyond your own gravity, and I can think of nothing else which can work that magic.

Consider that magic. There are stars and planets in the sky that can impart to you the secret of how many miles it is to safety: isn't that the most remarkable thing? Then there's our own sun, which we think of as nothing more than a warming friend, but through the regular passage of hours it helps define where you are on the surface of the earth. Isn't that magic, too? I wished I had a better understanding of the stars, the way they move, how they make the mathematical music that underscores the work of the traditional navigator. I have a sense of it, even if I can't explain it fully to you, and I have some sympathy for St Augustine when he said, "What then is time? If no one asks me, then I know what it is. If I wish to explain it to him who asks, I do not know."

You need a sextant, a watch, a set of tables as thick as an encyclopedia, and a clear head and calm frame of mind. Without the last two, you will get nowhere. You also need strong glasses if there is the slightest deficiency in your eyesight; also a sharp pencil and a finely honed patience, together with a sense of resignation to ease the frustration when your calculations suggest your sweltering ship is positioned somewhere inside the Arctic Circle. I bought a cheap, quartz-driven watch to keep time and set it to the pips before I left. When I later checked it against the time signal broadcast by the BBC World Service, it had lost only one second in five months. Harrison, the eighteenth-century creator of the ship's chronometer, would have wept at how easy it has all become. Beware lethargy. It is the astro-navigator's worst enemy. In the tropics there is more often sun than not, and so it is easy to excuse yourself and leave the taking of a sight for another day.

I used to "shoot" the sun, as taking a sight is called, from the cockpit, scribbling with one hand while whipping off my reading glasses to glance at the clock, then putting them back on to read the scale on the sextant. After a few wildly ridiculous results, I learned to spend more effort on carefully reading the time and the sextant's micrometer. Then I would go below to the heat of the cabin, often above 30°C, and cook my brain a little more with the steamy calculations, sweat flowing like a stream from the end of my nose on to the pages of minutely printed numbers before me. The first time I tried it, my technique blunted by years of little practice, it took me a full hour to "reduce the sight", as it's called. My rusty, superheated brain was stretched beyond its comfort zone by the need to do arithmetic to base sixty when dealing with time, but to base ten when averaging the minutes — the sextant is read in minutes and decimals of minutes, rather than seconds. There is much scope for arithmetical error. Nor is there a definitive result with just one observation of the sun, since all your efforts will only deliver a position line that stretches the complete circumference of the earth and all you know for certain is that you are somewhere on it. To get a fix you need at least two observations, and the more the better — perhaps the sun and a planet, or a planet and a star at twilight when you still have an horizon to measure against. I chose to leave the moon out of it for the moment; I was told its relatively faster motion adds to the arithmetical complexity, and quite honestly I was afraid of it.

But why bother at all? Because I enjoyed the extra-terrestrial connection and believe that there is much that is written in the sky that we might never understand. I became no longer an observer of the mysteries of the universe, but a participant. I was making my own contribution to my wellbeing and the safety of my little ship by finding my way by the stars. It was a truly out-of-this-world experience.

I have felt differently about the stars since Nicholas died. Were we shocked when Nicholas took his life? Or course we were, at first. I was at sea back in 2006, somewhere off the foggy coast of Nova Scotia after a singlehanded passage across the north Atlantic, when in a bleak spot I took the bleakest possible call on the satellite phone. Boat and voyage abandoned in an unexpected place, I was home within 24 hours. Although my wife, daughter and I were awash in utter grief, I soon found a force more powerful took control. There was a sense of deep peace and understanding, and no desire to play the pointless game of "What if . . .?" No guilt, no blame. Such things seemed disrespectful to Nicholas. He had made his choice. His startling mind, honed by the great love of poetry which took him through Oxford, had started to crumble, and an avalanche of profound mental illness was about to overtake him. He knew that, he sensed it coming at him like a rogue wave and chose to step aside. We could not blame him.

Over the painful weeks that followed, explanations started to drop into place. It started to seem less of a bolt from the blue. We arrived at a point of acceptance, agreeing that "it was written in the stars" and that, one by one, events were leading to an inevitable finale.

I thought of the dead, lots of them and not just Nicholas, and not in a maudlin way. I remembered with fondness sailors I had known who had been my inspiration and how they too had been drawn to these same unchanging skies and seen them not as a star-studded cloth but a tool with which they could find their way. What kind of a leap of imagination is that, and how brave, to deduce from a twinkle in the sky, via mathematics, to a pencil mark on a chart that tells you where you are?

When I first attempted astro-navigation forty years ago, when it was rather more relevant than today, my bible was a thin textbook written by Mary Blewitt, herself a top-class racing navigator in the 1950s. I did not know her, but knew a friend of hers well. Mike Richey was a supreme navigator, held in high regard, and at one time the director of the Institute of Navigation. A man precise in his manners and thought, he could use a sextant with the dexterity and certainty of a concert pianist approaching a Bechstein. I often thought about Mike while gazing at the stars. I first met him when he was well turned seventy but still voyaging in a crazy little boat called *Jester* — a 26-foot folkboat with a junk sail, which he described as "uncomfortable". Compared with the luxury of *Wild Song* it was decidedly monastic, which was what made it so appealing to Mike. It had no proper bunk, no decent galley, and a bucket for everything else. But simplicity was the attraction, and it was within these unlikely confines that he sailed the Atlantic alone thirteen times, the last crossing at the age of 82. I asked him how he coped with the long, repetitive days at sea and he replied, "I don't know. The time seems to pass." In truth, Mike helped time along a little, for his two sailing companions were the writings of St Paul and a decent quantity of red wine. He would have disapproved of my near teetotal approach, although I hope he might applaud my efforts with the sextant. He has been an inspiration to me.

I remember, in particular, a helpful remark he made at the very end of my own solo Atlantic crossing when I had just arrived in America. "You won't think much of it now, but it will grow on you." It proved true, and will again I expect. A passage under sail that seems routine at the time eventually moulds itself into a more profound experience. When we sail we are gathering the ingredients but the cake itself takes time to bake. We need that perspective to understand what our voyaging is really all about. If someone had asked me what I was making of the trip so far, and what impression it was having on me, I would probably have shrugged. I felt indifferent towards it. It was just a job — get the sails up, set the course, get it done, arrive in one piece, go home on the first flight. But as I write, time has passed since I sat under those stars and a fresh perspective grows. It slowly dawns that on those tropical nights there were many profound moments, if only slightly felt at the time. To see the sky laid out before you in such a concentrated way, to be given a view of it that is only possible when alone in the middle of a dark ocean, is to suddenly know that the breadth of human knowledge that feels so rich and confident on the shore evaporates into nothing when at sea. Yet it is nothing to fear, for it can only lead to the thought that anything is possible.

Some feel release when at sea but I didn't, not always. Compared to the heavens, the sea itself at times felt very limiting. From my point of view, I was living in a merely two-dimensional world. I could neither rise above it, nor did I wish to sink beneath it. I craved to know what it was like to be up amongst the stars, and yearned to understand the depths of the ocean, if that could be achieved without too close an examination. I concluded that to be on this ocean was not really a freedom at all, but might be an imprisonment. All I could do was drift along where sea met sky, and go no further. At times I was unable to see it as glorious freedom, and often I felt more trapped out there, under a tropical sky, than I have ever felt on land.

To return, for a moment, to St Augustine, who knew what time was but if pressed could not describe it — I feel the same way if asked about Nicholas and what sort of person he was. He was our beloved son with long, curly brown locks, a face that broke easily into a beguiling grin, with a subtle but enthusiastic sense of humour and a deep generosity of spirit. But that is the easy bit to describe. You could pretty much get all that from a photograph. If you pressed me, as Augustine was, for a deeper understanding, I might flounder. As I write, it is seven years since his death and the enigma has yet to be fully unravelled. Of one thing I am clear, though — I understand perfectly well why he took his life.

Here's my explanation. Something profound happened to Nicholas on his passage through school, and in his teens it brought him to literature. It might have been one book, one teacher, one brainwave that did it, I don't know. As a child he was a lover of stories, but most children are; he sketched silly poems on long journeys, but so do many others. So whatever force made literature a plank in his life and inspired him to create his own must have been a potent inspiration.

Alongside this must be set an unusual character. He was all the things I described above, but more. He spent long times alone, always outside the crowd, often wearing a troubled brow. His imagination, which was his most powerful possession, was also his burden. He would worry and never share it so his troubles were rarely halved, only multiplied by self-containment. As I write that, I realise that the same could have been said about me, for I was a lonely child at school — the one who always stood on the edge of the playground — and I was now pursuing the loneliest of travels. But we solo travellers are not always led to destruction, and indeed Nicholas found a paradoxical mix of insularity and comradeship in the crewing of a tall ship, which provided some of the best moments in his life. It is never far from my mind, though, that his desire to be apart from others and not one of the gang might be an unlucky result of the fall of the paternal genetic dice.

None of this might have mattered if his brain had maintained its travels on a straight and narrow path. I am sociable enough if I need to be, and if I want time to myself I take it. That's how we loners manage. But in Nicholas's case there were also signs of growing mental disorder — withdrawal, self-harming, compulsive exercise — his brain was taking its own path and was running out of his control. He lost the ability to concentrate on lengthy novels and took to more compact poetry. He knew there was something about himself that he was losing.

The coroner's verdict, that he killed himself "while the balance of his mind was disturbed", seems to me to be a perfect expression of what happened. Those who cannot comprehend the taking of one's own life — "Why would anyone want to do that?" — have not fully considered the meaning of those eight simple yet profound words. At the time of the final act, I have no doubt that to him it seemed the most reasonable and right thing to do. That's how disturbed minds are. And that was perhaps his greatest fear: that his well-controlled mind would soon lead him to places he had no wish to be as mental ill-health turned it inside out. And what use would his mind be to him then? And who would he be without it? He was bright enough to be able to form these questions and make a pretty good guess at the answers. I cannot blame him for ducking his head beneath the overwhelming wave that was heading his way. It took guts. I have often heard suicide described as the "coward's way out" but to me it seems the bravest of all acts.

So there you have him at the time of his death. A handsome young man of twenty-three with a winning smile and a ready laugh, who loved adventure and fought to overcome the predispositions of childhood only to find that his greatest possession, his mind, was fast betraying him. That's how it was.

There is one question that never leaves my mind, and that is where is Nicholas now? There are times when I have felt his presence; not imagined but as a distinct feeling. Let me explain. It is possible to imagine a desert but you cannot make yourself feel the heat. I can visualise an iceberg but I do not shudder with the cold. Feelings and imaginings are distinct. I can well imagine what it would be like to be close to him again, but that is not the same as the far more powerful sensation of "feeling" him near. Thoughts and imaginings are easy to tell apart from real feelings. I can imagine, for example, what he might say if he were reading this over my shoulder right now. He would remark, kindly so as not to be hurtful, that it was "very interesting". I can hear him saying it. But that is in my imagination, I know that.

At some stage I believed I would get a clear and distinct feeling of him as my journey progressed. I hoped so, anyway. It would come out of the blue, as it has before. It might be this week, next year, a decade hence. And if it came it would be in the form of a few words that exploded in my head out of nowhere. They would not come when I am thinking about him. But they *will* come, and they cannot go unheard.

"Ah, that's a common symptom of grief — voices from the dead," the materially minded wise will mutter. "We have a good scientific explanation for it. It can be understood by neuroscientists. We can scan the brain and we can see . . ." And on they ramble with their self-satisfied scientific explanation. I used to believe them, but now I can laugh at them and their convictions, for it is only when you are under stars so sharp in the sky that to brush your finger over them might scar you that you understand that the sum total of human knowledge is so pathetically small that there is no one on earth qualified to doubt any idea about life or death. My guess, and your guess, is just as good as anyone else's.

I doubt the question "Where's Nicholas now?" will ever be answered by me. But I seriously doubt anyone will convince me that what remains of him is nowhere.

CHAPTER
SIX

TRADE WIND DAYS

*The morning runs
on, a springtime secret
through the avenues
and avenues which lure
all sound away*

Mornings did run on in a way that afternoons did not. I soon became accustomed to rising with the sun, for its glare even at sunrise was too strong to ignore. The first hour of the day I spent in a daze, but soon focused on breakfast and thought about jobs which that must be done that day — vegetable locker checked, then water tanks, followed by diesel. Afternoons were more problematical, and when the going was easy this was the time I would get bored. The afternoons provided time for thought, though.

What are "*the avenues and avenues which lure all sound away*"? Were these the pathways of the night down which the morning silently creeps, as welcome as spring with its secret promise of better times ahead? I let such thoughts loose and let them swirl around. Nothing more.

★　★　★

A few hundred miles only to the Cape Verdes, according to the GPS, the satellite navigator that gives generously with one hand but takes plenty with the other in return. With apparent generosity, it will tell you the distance to go, and even worse it will give you an ETA, Estimated Time of Arrival. It is impossible not to become obsessed with it as it creates a sense of urgency that has no place in your life. It is making your voyage across the unconfined ocean about as enjoyable as a morning commute to the radio accompaniment of time checks. But you can't ignore it. You are in a paradoxical position because you are as close to a sensation of suspended time as you can possibly be — perhaps the nearest you will ever get to a feeling of eternity — but the dancing numbers try at every turn to wreck the experience. Switch it off! I've done that in the past, but always switched the damned thing back on again within a few hours. And for what purpose? What does it matter precisely where I am? I am where I am.

As dusk fell after a day of calm during which a few hours of engine use had made the cabin unbearably hot, the joy of pulling the stop lever was as great as release from a straitjacket. The rattle of it confines all thought to a tiny corner of your head where ideas have no space to move around. I even find it difficult to read when the engine is on, so that first minute after the engine stops and as the boat slows and resumes her familiar shakes and rattles and the sails fill, when the sound of the sea lapping against the hull becomes the predominant noise, is a heavenly time. It matters not in the slightest that your speed has dropped a couple of knots and that the infernal ETA has moved back by a couple of days. You are aware once again of where you are and what is around you. Jupiter, I noticed, was rising, but it was too dark to attempt a sight. You need a clear horizon against which to measure altitude. She looked so tempting, and so powerful. I vowed she would not escape me again, and the next time she dared to show her face I would be ready for her with my sextant. She can run the entire width of the heavens, but she can't hide.

I was now at 22 degrees north with Mauritania the nearest land some 300 miles to the east. The moon rose as dusk was falling and kept me company through the night. It was quite full, and in the depths of midnight filled the cockpit with light, almost bright enough to read by. Its rising and setting, of course, changed as the days passed; but for the best part of a week its appearance seemed to coincide with the business of getting ready for the long, tropical night and I greeted it every evening like a returning friend.

My own glow, my masthead light which betrays my presence to other ships, still did not work. I stared up at what should be its red, green and white beacon and saw only darkness. But even when working, to set its feeble glow against the brilliance of the stars seemed such a futile gesture that I wasn't bothered. I'd take my chances. It was pretty deserted out here with not one ship seen since the Canaries. I devoured one pot of the remaining two Ambrosia rice puddings and a content evening followed.

Not a scrap of wildlife came calling in those first weeks. Neither bird nor fish, whale nor dolphin. Nothing. You could easily believe this was a planet entirely devoid of creatures other than me. If I were to stand on the foredeck and holler, "Is there anybody out there?", there would be no reply. There wasn't even a jellyfish blobbing along. On a trip to the Azores I became bewitched by the sight of wise old turtles slowly paddling their way along the world's ocean currents, making a stately and untroubled progress of the kind I envied, but not even one of those old geezers paid a call. I had identification books on board, serious tomes which covered every marine species known to man, but nothing showed itself and there was no need to turn the pages. Until one morning, when the first flying fish landed on deck. It was a pathetic little scrap so small that even a cat wouldn't have shown any interest. It was dead, of course, having chosen a bad moment to launch itself into the air and land in the scuppers rather than the ocean. I have heard of flying fish so large they can give the helmsman a swipe round the head. Not this little mite.

Our speed was dropping again. I am no bone-between-the-teeth type, but 1.8 knots was too slow even for me. It was becoming increasingly hot by day, only cooling a degree or so by night, and the thought of any exertion was too much to contemplate. Then I remembered that I had not touched a rope or a winch handle for the last two days. I had allowed myself to become a prisoner to idleness, content to be wafted along at an unspectacular 3 knots. It was time for me to set the pace. I set the colourful MPG, a red and yellow multipurpose genoa, and with a little more breeze we were back up to 3 knots and all was well with the world. Except it wasn't entirely a happy ship, for I felt the weight of the calendar pressing down on my shoulders and was uncertain how long the remaining leg down from the Cape Verdes would take. I did some calculations, measured distances, counted the days on the calendar and did some long divisions, and concluded that I might not have time to stop there after all. Wouldn't it be better to press on? That is what I might have done had I not undertaken an inspection of the dwindling fruit and veg and found that the three large white cabbages were showing severe rot. White cabbages, as hard as footballs, are impervious to anything nature can throw at them: you cannot bruise them, drown them, nor impact upon them in any way except with a sharp knife. But now, in a steamy sub-tropical atmosphere, they had met their match. If only for the sake of getting something fresh on board, a stop at Cape Verde was compulsory.

Having made that decision, I settled down to run the last hundred miles. A ship came into sight, not far away, clearly heading towards me. On yet another gadget I can get a display of its course, speed, distance off, danger of collision, what the crew are having for supper (not really) and, most interestingly, its destination. I gave a wry smile when I read that she was bound for Falmouth. She would eat up the miles back to home in a way I never could. I watched her disappear over the horizon and thought that it would not be many days before she had sight of the lovely Lizard peninsula and the cliff-fringed coast of Cornwall and the green fields beyond. For tuppence I'd have hitched a ride home.

I was distracted from that thought by the sight of a shoal of flying fish, a good twenty or more of them flitting from wave to wave. It is the most beautiful spectacle, especially when seen with the setting sun behind them. Then their wings refract the rays, making rainbows, and they become more a trick of the light than a sea creature.

A thought occurred as I watched them bounce across the sea: an ordinary fish does not know that it swims in water. Only we, the outside observers, can know that. It has known nothing but water around itself since it came into being, and will probably know no better until the day it dies. It does not sense that there is another world beyond, has no reason to suspect. Then, one day, it is caught in a fisherman's net and hauled from the water into the alien air and daylight and discovers there is another place. By which time it is too late. To make that profound discovery it must die.

But the flying fish is different. It steals a glimpse of a different world every time it leaps, and so it knows that there is more to life than being surrounded by water. It has that special gift of being able to see beyond itself. Writers, poets and artists have talents which give them the ability to envisage and describe what the rest of us cannot see. Nicholas was a writer and a poet and was given the glimpse of another place, and through his writing told us what he saw. He leapt, in his mind, from one world to another. Just like the flying fish, from its world into ours, and back again.

Where were those bloody islands? The electronics said only 23 miles to go. On a clear day I might have seen them from 50 miles off, but there was not a thing in sight. It was nearly five o'clock and the day was beginning to ebb. Then an outline of a craggy mountain top snapped into view, followed by the hazy shape of an island, quite close, looking like a cardboard cut-out so sharp you could shave with it. It was now dusk, which falls quickly at these latitudes. Reassured that the chart showed two bright lighthouses on the tips of each island, I was then deflated to read in the pilot book that the navigation lights were often not working. Complete darkness now. No light shone. A few twinkles on the hillsides betrayed dwellings but no beam to lead me kindly and safely into harbour.

The wind fell away, but the warmth it had accumulated as it travelled across the sandy wastes of Mauritania was enough to have me dripping in sweat late into the evening. I started to motor in the blackness, totally reliant on the GPS (which had turned friend now) because I could make out no shore on either side. It was fortunate that the instruments were going through a phase of playing the game and I was able to stab the autopilot button while I darted from chart to helm and back again. The approach looked good on paper. It was time to grope my way in, setting the engine to give us a slow but safe 2 knots, which would give me ample time to do the close quarters navigation and not create too much of a dent if we hit anything. The pilot book sternly warned that this was not a safe place to approach in the dark. I was buggered if I was going back to sea.

We were out of the ocean swell now in perfect windless shelter, and slowly street lights and houses started to appear. From behind a headland shone the bright, inviting loom of a large town, Mindelo. I switched on the radar. I rarely do so, because it is an instrument out of which I have rarely been able to get a decent tune, but on this occasion it showed the coast clearly and distinctly and I felt safe proceeding, reassured that a large, unlit rock ahead had ceased to be an indistinct smudge and was now a distinct green blob on the radar screen. Helpfully, the floodlights on the docks were casting enough light across the water for me to see any unlit fishing boats, of which there could be plenty.

My nerve left me when I was almost within reach of the anchorage. By our position on the chart, and all the other indicators, the anchorage off the town's waterfront should be just round the next corner. But I felt unsure, distracted by a throng of ghostly, abandoned ships anchored in the bay, near wrecks and not a coat of paint between them. A sign was all I wanted. Just one bloody signal that would confirm I was in the right place and would not have to spend the night in that graveyard.

A red light! A solitary flashing red light on the end of a pier had been, until now, obscured by the lights of a cargo ship moored alongside. I turned to close on it, and as I came around the stern of yet another rusting hulk the masts of gathered yachts appeared. I glanced at the echo sounder, which was measuring the depth of water beneath us, and edged closer to the shore till it felt right to anchor. I sprinted forward and let the anchor go, then back to the cockpit to watch as we drifted backwards in the light breeze. The tightening of the anchor chain eventually sent that satisfying jolt through the boat that tells you that you have made connection with the land once again.

It was midnight, the air completely still. The only sound was the buzz of a distant ship's engine. I took out the Cape Verde national flag and as a courtesy hoisted it from the starboard spreader. I wondered what kind of welcome the dawn would bring.

CHAPTER
SEVEN

CAPE VERDE

I was woken by the rising sun, refreshed after an unbroken night's sleep, to find the breeze had freshened: the same north-east wind that had brought me all the way from Europe — the self-same driving force for centuries of exploration under sail.

I scanned the waterfront, tea in hand, just looking, and enjoying the satisfaction of arrival. I saw straight away that Mindelo had no high-rise buildings and no slums either. It was not what you would call a scrubbed facade, but it had certainly had its face well washed. Although 350 miles off the African coast, and referred to as an African state, it didn't look like it. I was expecting a ramshackle kind of place. It is not many years since visiting yachts reported theft, pilfering and pickpocketing, but I noticed a couple in their smart new rubber dinghy, complete with shiny outboard, simply drive it on to the beach and walk away as if it was as safe as in their own back garden. Things must have changed. White houses spread up the dusty hillsides; the familiar sign of a Shell filling station shone out like a beacon on the waterfront, emphasising that this place looks as much to Europe for support as to nearby Africa.

The romantic streak within me says that a proper landfall in a foreign country is undertaken in a rowing dinghy and your first footfall is on to a sandy beach. Marinas steal that magical moment from you, as this one was about to. After a long sail, the offer of comfort and security is too much to shun. Mountaineers returning from a summit do not pitch a tent when there is chance of a hot shower in a nearby B&B. Likewise, sailors are seduced by marinas, as I was.

I came alongside the fuel pumps and asked if there was someone to help me berth. No sooner had the jovial girl put down the phone than three boys with shiny black faces and enormous grins came running down the pontoon as if some kind of party was about to kick off. One leapt on the stern, the other two went to the bow and gave me a wave to head off. I did what I was told by the ten-year-old now in charge at the bow. We headed into a vacant berth and with a giant leap the two lads on the bow were ashore and making off the lines. Another appeared with an even broader grin on his face and picked up a stern line and handed it to me. I made it fast. We were perfectly secure. Should they get a tip? They were standing on the walkway looking at me and I wondered if that thought was going through their minds. They had certainly earned it, and if reports of the standard of living here were correct they would probably appreciate it. I went below to get a few dollar notes but by the time I came back up they were gone. Later, when it was time to leave, I did force some money on them but it was not asked for and not expected.

Crime is now scarce here and tourists and sailors are not harassed. The marina owner, a German, Kai Brosman, must take some of the credit for a major change in the fortunes of this mid-Atlantic speck. Having spotted an increase in transatlantic sailing traffic to the Caribbean, and realising that Cape Verde was a good stopping-off place, Brosman decided a marina development would be good business. But the criminal ways of the lads who frequented the waterfront were against him. He cut a deal. He said to the lads that without the visiting yachts, who bring money which they spend in shops and restaurants, everyone is worse off. "So, you stop the thieving," he said, "and I will train you how to work in a marina and make you into *marinieros*, then I pay you a proper wage and then you don't need to thieve. How about it?" The German did good. I guess the insistent pestering by the many prostitutes as you walk from the marina into the town he considered one campaign too far.

Everything you could wish for can be found in Mindelo, but you have to look for it. One shop would have bread but no butter; when you found butter there was no milk; when you found milk yet another shop would provide jam. Fresh meat looked far too much like a road accident to contemplate, but was doubtless wholesome. Everyone seemed young and full of life. This is a famously youthful nation where the elderly stand out as distinctly as Granddad at a disco. The middle-aged were not in evidence. I gave a few coins to a man with a white stick who sat on a doorstep, eyes closed as if empty. He held out a hand. As the coins trickled into his palms I noticed he looked down to count them. Not all their cunning has departed them.

What a strange sight I must have presented as I staggered out of a hardware store with two plastic nappy buckets, one in each hand, swaying my way back to the boat on legs still not used to the unyielding nature of pavements. I felt a need to explain that this lone sailor required nappy buckets to make into devices for stopping the turbine of his water-driven generator from spinning when he tried to recover it. I don't suppose they would have believed me.

I spent three days in the harbour and everyone of them was filled with shopping, administration, refuelling, watering, maintenance, until the act of going back to sea felt like a holiday. I did not see the far side of the island, or climb a hill, or ride a bus to the mountains. I was just too busy. I had not left enough time for recreation. On the first afternoon I sought out the immigration office and walked in crippling heat along the waterfront to the commercial docks, unsure amidst the sea of black faces which country or even continent I was in. The office was by the dock gates and the place hummed with drifters and idlers, or crews waiting for their ships to come in. It was that general drift to and fro that is the mark of harbours the world over. I pushed my way through an amiable crowd, getting occasional glances of suspicion as if I might be about to steal work they had been waiting weeks for, and finally found the uniformed, gun-carrying official I was seeking. When asked my previous port, I lied and told them it was Morocco and showed the exit stamp in my passport from that country. I had neither the will nor the language to explain the absence of officials on the island of Lanzarote. He didn't look as though he would have cared either way.

Most people here appeared to have serious cruising intentions; getting here takes more than a little effort, and getting anywhere else from here takes a substantial one, so that was no surprise. People are often like their boats in shape and temperament. A blond German man of vast physical proportions had a broad and unwieldy catamaran to match his bulk, painted yellow to match his hair. His preoccupation was the speed of his broadband connection. There were other big catamarans too, mostly French and very stylish, with highly perfumed women on board who draped themselves across the afterdeck like wisps of sailcloth. Amidst the obvious wealth, though, was a young man on a ramshackle boat, dressed in tattered shorts, striding the peeling deck of his painted and rotting wooden boat. He was staring towards the sky with a look in his eye, imagining he was Moitessier, perhaps. He would not be away any time soon.

Just as that thankful moment arrived when the sun finally dipped beneath the mountain top of the distant island and it became safe to emerge from under the sunshade and take a cold beer, there was a hesitant tap on the foredeck. A young lad from the marina stood with an apologetic look on his face. He said that he had earlier boarded my boat without permission, and he was very sorry. I asked why. He said it had been to return the card key I had left behind in the showers earlier in the day. I did not see anything in that act of kindness that required an apology and told him so. I grew to love those kids who worked in that marina.

My first afternoon back at sea turned into near disaster. The land soon disappeared behind misty air made dusty by the Saharan sand blown on the trade wind. I made a southerly course with 2,000 miles to go to Brazil. The wind, I thought, was pretty much where it always had been, from the north-east, and so I set my favourite rig, which was the mainsail and the lightweight multipurpose genoa supported by a pole to leeward. As I came out of the shelter of the islands the wind shifted a little, as it always does when you creep out of the shadow of land, but I failed to realise this. Instead, I thought the sail was not set properly, which explained its failure to fill with wind. I decided the luff needed to be tighter so I went to the mast and, filled with the enthusiasm that departure gives you, gave it two mighty turns on the winch. By six o'clock, with the sun beginning to set, the sail still refused to behave. It was only then that I realised it was a problem with the wind, not with the sail. The wind had merely shifted. Why I did not work this out sooner I cannot imagine. If I got rid of the pole and sheeted the sail conventionally, all would be well. To achieve this I first needed to drop the sail.

I went to the mast and released the halyard holding up the sail. Nothing moved. I pulled and tugged but nothing gave. I went to the bow and swung on the sail with all my weight, but again nothing budged. The sail was stuck to the masthead and flogged in a rising wind. This was beyond my experience. I had never had things stick at the top of masts before. A moment of panic set in as I scrambled to come up with a way of bringing the sail down. I grabbed the binoculars and lay flat on the deck, trying to see what had jammed at the masthead, but I couldn't hold them steady enough to learn much. When I did finally get a glimpse it was far from clear what was wrong. I am not prone to blind panic but I was sufficiently close to it this time. I even thought of ringing home to ask what I should do.

There were few options. Should I call the marina? It was Saturday night. What chance they could help me now? A pathetic response, anyway. For a short while I tried to head back under engine, but with a head wind and sea and a full sail flapping up front the engine soon overheated at the effort.

Over a cup of tea inspiration came, as it so often does. I opened the drawer of the chart table and pulled out a surgically sharp sailing knife, a present from my daughter at Christmas. I went to the foredeck, taking with me a length of line. With a heavy heart I made an incision in the lovely sail about two feet above the deck and directly over the powerful anchor winch. It felt like a violent attack on an old friend. Round the luff of the sail I tied the rope with a rolling hitch and brought it down to the winch. I stabbed the button and the powerful winch turned, the fabric of the sail started to stretch and there was the sound of tearing. Even the winch, more used to hauling the weighty anchor chain, started to labour as it exerted all the force it was capable of. Then a cascade of red and yellow cloth fell about me and the sail was down. I fought my way out of it like a man who had got on the wrong side of the drapes during a curtain call. I grappled the rest of it out of the water, bundled it into its bag and screamed with joy. It became clear, on examining the halyard, that with brute force and disregard I had winched the long, fat, tapered splice into the tight cheeks of the masthead block, where it had swollen and jammed. Lesson learnt. I set the simple genoa, raised the pole to support it, and by the time full darkness was on us we were making 7 knots and heading due south towards the next milestone, the equator.

CHAPTER
EIGHT

DOLDRUM DAYS

Ahead lay the infamous doldrums, an area north of the equator where the trade winds, blowing in opposite directions, cancel each other out, leaving you with a no-man's-land kind of weather where the default option is calm. If this voyage were to be described as a drama, you would say the first act had been played out against the background of the north-east trades and the second act, the doldrums, was about to begin.

The first sign that things were changing was lightning in the night: vivid and disturbing sheet lighting danced between black clouds in all directions, at all levels, bright enough to cast shadows in the cockpit but distant enough to cause no sound of thunder. The clouds came into backlit relief as the atmospheric sparks intensified, but the wind remained steady and the sea calm. I had read of tropical squalls which bring winds that go from calm to gale force within a minute and release downpours so torrential that they are painful on the skin. I rather fancied a bit of that, just for a change. I decided to take in some sail although the wind was still light, just in case. Within a few minutes it had freshened to force four — hardly threatening — and then moved ahead so that I had to winch in the headsails and mainsail, and quickly come to terms with the fact that I now had a boat that was sailing close to the wind; an experience this voyage had so far failed to offer. Soon I could no longer lay the course and so I tacked, trimmed the sheets and set off on a new course as the rain started to fall. I longed for it to be torrential and be a true tropical experience, but it failed me and fell into the heavy shower category with no more than a fresh breeze for all of fifteen minutes. Once that was gone I was left in a near calm, slopping along. It was a pathetic weakling of a tropical squall, an idle sod of a thing. To add to the disappointment, I realised that over an energetic half hour I had sailed in a complete circle, made no progress, and experienced insufficient of a downpour to qualify me as a Man of the Tropics. Next time, I vowed I would ignore the squalls and let them pass, like you do when rowdy kids are kicking a ball down the street: not worth getting worked up about because it won't be long before it's quiet again.

There is something about a doldrum sky that is deeply disturbing — the dark clouds hover like troubled souls, packed with potential drama but with little subsequent action. They are all trailer but no big picture. Through the doldrum days I watched towering masses build from dark and threatening bases high into the powder blue sky, but little ever resulted. Only one shower was heavy enough to rid the boat of a salt cake that was clinging to everything on deck.

I could still not fathom how one place on an ocean feels different to another. Some days I felt quite at home and relaxed where I was; I felt as though I had lived there all my life and it seemed as comforting as home. Yet I could sail 20 miles and start to feel uneasy, although nothing observable or tangible had changed. On land it is easy to define what is comforting and what offers threat: rugged mountains inspire, foggy days depress, sunshine on green fields lifts the heart, morning dew on roses makes the spirit rise, icy roads make you careful. On the ocean you can experience the same sensations, although obvious stimuli are lacking. Perhaps the ocean needs us to possess a sense of the subtle to be understood. And peace of mind too. My head seemed filled with noise, overwhelmingly so, and the kind of creative thought that leads to real understanding remained beyond my reach.

The Cape Verde long-life milk proved lousy and soon smelled of fish. Their bread turned into pretty grim stuff too, prone to instant mildew, unlike the Canary Islands loaves which lasted a week. The cucumber was bitter and the tomatoes tasteless even when doused in dressing. Little joy was to be expected from the galley now. Oranges kept well, though, and I rationed myself to one every morning on waking. Apples that seemed sound one day would be mush by the next. Even the onions started to wilt, and the potatoes soon turned putrid, giving off the vilest scent known to man short of rotting flesh. It was after a thorough, sick-making clearance of the fresh food locker that I decided to use some of the precious water to take my first cockpit shower, which proved such a treat that it became a daily habit, usually taken just before dark and looked forward to all day, making a much anticipated punctuation mark. How lost we are without markers in the day.

Nicholas and I spent a jolly hour together — he the spirit and me the poor sod with a needle and thread in his hand — as I repaired the wound I had deliberately inflicted on the genoa in order to retrieve it from the masthead. The joke centred around a "Handy Stitcher", a device I knew had tormented him over many hours on his tall ships expeditions while repairing sails. I remember him groaning at the memory of the hours he spent labouring over folds of canvas with this infuriating sewing device in his hand. It is a fiddly little tool that requires much pushing and shoving in order to make a single stitch and is quite tricky to get right even with the flimsy sailcloth I was trying to mend. What it must have been like for him to have to attack heavy, tall ship canvas I cannot imagine. Unlike a conventional father-son relationship, where it is the parent who is the calm and steadying influence, I always felt it was the opposite in our case. And so while I stitched and sweated and bled from my finger ends and felt generally cross with the world, the loudest voice in my head was his reminding me that this was the lot of sailors down the generations, and that frustration and fatigue must be controlled because all that mattered was a sound and strong result. Such a shame that someone possessed of such a proper frame of mind should eventually lose it.

I sewed all morning under a blazing sun, fingers too stiff and sore to lift a mug of tea after a full four hours of passing the waxed thread backwards and forwards through the cursed cloth. When it was done, and a passable if unusual repair had been made with a square of canvas stolen from an old hatch cover, the sail looked sound and ready to hoist. I wanted to ask Nicholas what he thought of the job I'd done. In this lonely, mid-ocean world where sense and reason can leave you and the impossible seems real, you easily believe that you are able to talk again, laugh and cry, be together. The only thing missing is that you can never reach out and touch, but for a short while you can do without that. Then comes the most hurtful of all moments, when you are shaken by cruel reality, when the distance between you becomes real. He is not here in the cockpit, on the ocean, sailing with me. He is gone. And now my stomach tightens as the finality of that overtakes me for the umpteenth time. But for hours past he has been as alive in my thoughts as if he were sitting next to me. That is the best I can hope for now, and I must be satisfied and not complain. Yet what does it matter if he is dead or alive, for such a differentiation is made with human eyes. There might be another way of looking at things.

Some people tell me they fear the vastness of the ocean, but those who are wary of the idea of eternity should sit for days on end in the doldrums. As the sun scorches and winds prove fickle, you realise that the distance between then, now and forever is not huge, and that is why I am certain that my separation from

Nicholas and all that he was is truly paper thin; so thin at times that we can still share a joke while stitching sailcloth.

In the early hours of the morning, when still dark, I saw a distant ship approaching from astern. I had seen several over the previous hours and assumed I was crossing a shipping lane between Africa and the Americas. All had passed wide of me but this one appeared to be behaving differently. I could see both his navigation lights, one red, the other green, and both his masthead lights were in line. In other words, he was steering straight at me. I have a device that emits a radio signal guaranteed to shine bright on a ship's radar screen. I checked it was switched on and working, which it was. Still he ploughed on, the distance between us getting ever less.

It would have been a simple thing to alter course, start the engine and power out of his way, but I was flying the newly restored genoa supported by a pole, which limited my scope for manoeuvre. I gave a call on the VHF radio and in as insistent a voice as I could manage called, "*Securitay . . . Securitay. Southbound ship, this is yacht* Wild Song *dead ahead of you. Over.*" No response. His lights grew brighter, his course unwavering, his bow now pointing directly at my stern and only a mile away. Tropical lightning filled the sky and frozen in the brief flashes I could now make out the distinct outline of the small coaster. Collision was now a real threat. Should I dramatically alter course? With my headsail flying from its pole I could easily end up with no control and then I would be a sitting duck. As I ran a check list in my head of how to launch the liferaft, what to throw in it, every bloody thing I could think of, a dark voice came on the radio. "I see you," it growled. Slowly the ship altered course and ran close down our port side. She looked like a rusty relic from the 1950s light cargo trade. Her engines thumped and her stack threw out heavy black smoke. Caught in the flashes of lightning I could see she was painted white, but a long time ago. Broad streaks of brown ran from her decks to the waterline. She had the look of a little ship that was up to no good and I was relieved when she steamed out of sight.

For the next couple of days the mild-mannered breeze rose and fell with a rhythm like the warm breath of a loved one lying next to you. Although it showed signs of tiredness it never failed entirely, which gave me hope that although I might be making a slow passage south I was not going to be brought to a complete halt and becalmed for days on end, as generations before me have suffered.

I started to need less sleep and felt some weight disappearing. Food was rapidly becoming less appetising. In cooler climes, I thought it a good trick to prepare a large meal in the pressure cooker, enough for two nights, to save having to cook two days on the run. But when I married tuna with the last couple of decent potatoes and a chunk or two of chorizo (which seemed to have lasted all the way from Portugal so God knows what was in it), with some other random stuff chucked in, I had a delicious meal the first night and replaced the lid tightly. A mere twelve hours later, a putrid, determined stench was fighting its way out of the sealed pan. On opening it, with the nervousness of a man defusing a land mine, I found the contents well on their way to obnoxious slime.

Then the wind really died. I don't mean it dropped, or fell away, it just died a sudden death. I was filled with a profound feeling that there might never be wind again. I took a measure of the fuel in the tank. I could afford to motor for twenty-four hours — no more. I would have to steer by hand, with the electric autopilot no longer wishing to come out and play. It was breakfast time. I brewed some tea, lathered myself with suncream, found a wide-brimmed hat and settled down for a long old slog.

It turned out not too bad. Providing you are comfortable, then time seems to pass. By lunchtime the heat of the sun was almost unbearable, even through clothes, and I noticed that for no reason at all the sea was becoming rough, which could not have been due to the wind, for there was none. Out of nowhere appeared waves with curling tips, just like tide rips, and swirls and eddies caught us and tried to throw us from side to side. I could not get out of my head the idea that we were sailing uphill, although this was clearly nonsense. Then, from the south-east, came the first hint of a swell. Nothing much to start with, just the slightest rise and fall which grew as the hours passed till by evening it was a distinct and unmistakably regular motion of the sea. For there to be swell, there must be wind, even if some miles away. This I craved, for when it appeared it would get hold of me by the scruff of the neck and haul me out of the doldrums and send me on my way. Before dark, a ripple started to appear on the surface of the sea, often the harbinger of a waft of air seen long before it is felt. The mainsail started to creep across the boat, yielding to the breeze's growing pressure. The flag at the masthead started to lift, and a cooling on my cheek confirmed that the wind was back. I gave a cheer. The boat rose from her torpid ways and breathed a sigh of relief. From her stern came the chuckle of water going past; she was singing with joy in her voice. We were on our way again. This was surely the first hint of the trade wind. It had to be.

CHAPTER
NINE

ACROSS THE EQUATOR
TO BRAZIL

No sooner had that wind started to blow than it felt like being back in the English Channel, it really did. The air seemed fresher and more cooling; the boat had a liveliness that I had not felt for weeks as she started to take the waves on her shoulder rather than her backside. The trade winds are true wafts of freedom: a release from the imprisonment of our own continents, and from the grasp of the great weather systems that do their utmost to confine us.

Life aboard became more of a balancing act as I moved from handhold to handhold, grasping and reaching — something I had not needed to do for many weeks. Standing up required effort, resulting in more bunk-time, but when progress is good and in the right direction then small inconveniences, such as having to carefully place one's mug of tea, are of little matter. It felt so good to be on the move again that, irrespective of the already tropical cabin temperatures, I lit the oven and baked bread. The dough rose like a dream in the warmth and the smell rising from the oven inexplicably added to a sense of being in home waters.

Waypoint "Brazil" was a set of numbers I had punched into the GPS. It was a randomly chosen spot about a hundred miles off the bulge of the South American continent for which I now steered. But there is a problem, and that is the prominent tip of South America, Cape San Roque, and an ocean current, the Brazilian current, which flows strongly westwards from the African coast, driven by a more easterly trade wind to be found south of the equator. Where the massive flow of water meets the Brazilian landmass it divides, one leg heading north-westwards towards the Caribbean, and the other southwards towards Rio de Janeiro. It does not present much of a problem for a modern, weatherly sailing yacht, but in the days of trading under sail in unhandy ships it was all too easy to be caught by this current, carried north, thus failing to weather Cape San Roque. What this meant for the hapless ship trying to make its way from Europe to Cape Horn was a huge and wearisome circuit of the north Atlantic, possibly as far north as the Azores. It could take several months and thousands of miles of sailing just to get back to where you started. Hence the advice in a distinguished volume, published by the Admiralty, called *Ocean Passages for the World*. It warned that if faced with a southerly wind south of the doldrums, you should take the tack which would have you pointing at south Africa. But a modern yacht that can sail close to the wind is a different creature from an old tea clipper, so I made a beeline for my Brazilian waypoint and was relaxed about it.

The possibility occurred of taking another break. I was just three degrees north of the equator, and it was now only 400 miles to the island of Fernando de Noronha, which would be five days' sailing at most. Once the thought of land enters your head it becomes overpowering. It is difficult to explain how it is possible to love being on the ocean while at the same time yearning to be off it. After a fortnight at sea I was relishing the prospect of a tropical island. Who wouldn't?

To the last few leaves of cabbage I added meatballs that night, and while sitting in the cockpit and devouring my meal I spotted a distant white sail astern of me on the starboard side. I watched it for some while, just to check it wasn't an illusion, for to see another yacht in such unfrequented waters seemed unlikely. I washed up, fiddled around a bit, and when I came back on deck I saw that, surprisingly, she was slipping astern and from sight. I say surprising because it is rare for me to be the fastest sailor in any such encounter; others always seem to have the longest legs. I altered course by about ten degrees to starboard so that our courses diverged even more. The last thing I needed was to be shadowed in the hours of darkness. Let's give each other some room. Soon they disappeared and I thought no more of them.

The huge moon that rose that night was as red as a tomato, I swear it. It had been a true friend as it had come and gone for the whole of this Atlantic passage so far, never failing to appear at some stage in the night and always welcome. It was diminishing now and soon the nights when it seemed to blaze from dusk to dawn would be gone. Whilst in a celestial frame of mind I put the clock back an hour, or was it forward? I am truly perplexed by time shifts and it unsettled me for several days. I have often pondered what it means to cross the International Date Line, that Pacific demarcation between one day and the next. You either have the same day twice, or miss a day, depending on which way you are going.

The next afternoon the trade wind faltered. It was heart-stopping, like a car suddenly running out of petrol. Then the GPS went on the blink for half an hour, bleeping with the cry of a lost child that couldn't find its satellites. This had never happened before. I did a lot of button stabbing and instruction-book reading, but we seemed to have sailed into some kind of dark place, like a black hole, where the wind didn't blow and the feeble little signals from satellites did not penetrate. Then the wind came back and the numbers on the screen sprang to life. I never did figure out what had happened, but was more than ready to accept there might be places on the planet where the usual rules don't apply.

Eventually I crossed the equator. It was the thirteenth of October. I had been looking forward to the moment for so long, yet when it arrived it hardly seemed to matter. Some voyagers make a great fuss of the business of "crossing the line" by dressing and partying, but I didn't feel the need. I'd crossed so many personal lines already. If I was sailing with a crew and a celebratory drink had been taken, it might have been a different matter, but alone it seemed better to let a small celebration happen in my head rather than launch an entire party for my own benefit. However, just in case all those customs have some point, I thought I'd take out a little insurance and pay Neptune some kind of homage. So, a drop of whisky was cast upon the waters, followed by a precious few crumbs of cake. That would have to do. It worked.

Later that night as I stood hypnotised beneath the glow of that ruddy moon, its rays so strong as to cast my shadow across the boat's cockpit, its sheer tropical brilliance was more intense than ever I remembered it before. Some say that being alone at sea adds to one's feeling of insignificance. I felt the exact opposite. I reached for my pen and scribbled in my diary, "*To stand beneath the moon and stars in the open ocean is not a measure of insignificance. It is a triumph. It is to achieve your own place within this cosmos, your very own place which is no other's. And you have done this by mastery of this crazy assemblage of wire and plastic and bits and pieces we call a boat. That is not insignificance — that is victory.*"

My one big concern about this trip was that smothering sadness would overtake me and I would have no one to share it with. I accepted Nicholas's death, and largely understood it, but to be alone for so long might open up fresh doubts and uncertainties with no guarantee that I could cope with them. I was not afraid if grief itself should return, though. In the weeks after his death, when sorrow submerges you, I found myself in a totally unexpected place, and not a challenging one either. I remember it as a time of great serenity, of awareness of all things natural, of sensitivity to all things that might be part of this world or even another. It gave birth to a desire for there to be only peace in every corner of the world; for there to be no cross words of any kind on any lips. It was not a time for tears, but for enlightenment; it was a time for insights. I look back on grief as a good thing to have lived through. Over time, of course, the intensity of the grief diminishes. Then comes the hardest bit, for the exalted place to which grief has taken you slowly falls back to earth, and then the real, hard slog begins.

Jupiter shone brightly that night, the most intense I had ever seen her, shedding light on new thoughts. This, I calculated, would be my last night at sea before landfall on a tropical island. I felt no real desire to stop and that this drift could go on for ever. But did I feel that only because I knew this leg was nearly over? Would I have felt the same if I had known that there were weeks of it stretching ahead? I think not. There is relaxation to be found in the realisation of things coming to an end. In the case of one's life, might briefness and consequent concentration of lifespan be a bonus? Of course, you would have to know that your life was going to be a short one. I wonder, then, if that is why, from an early age, Nicholas might have sensed his life was not to be a long one, and the composure that springs from that might have been the source of his perceptions far beyond a person of his few years?

★ ★ ★

What I now felt were my very own tropical islands, clear in the binoculars, were standing proud from the deep blue sea. I claimed ownership of them, feeling I had won them by my own efforts. There are, in fact, twenty-one islands in this group, which sit just 200 miles off the Brazilian coast, the nearest big city being Natal. Fernando de Noronha had been a prison island until as recently as 1945, and it is said you see no trees because the tropical forests were felled to prevent the prisoners from making rafts. As far as making my escape from the ever-present north-easterly swell was concerned, it was the main island that mattered and that is only 7 square miles. When a big swell is running, the shelter can be minimal and a stopover not worth the discomfort. I was lucky and the bay was calm. Part of this island sticks up like a sore thumb, a remnant of a volcanic plug, and is the first thing you see from seawards many miles off — a thumb's-up marking a good place to be.

To make the reconnection with the land is to risk a soaking here. Although the swell is not obvious, it exists nevertheless as a strong undertow, and the moment you step from the inflatable dinghy on to the shore your feet are swept from under you. I took a soaking in the pleasantly balmy sea, warmed by a current that flows all the way from Africa and brings sufficient heat for diving here to be possible to 50 metres without a wetsuit. I hauled the dinghy high above the waterline and tied it to a rusty old winch used to draw fishing boats above the high tide mark. The harbour itself is formed by a pier built of imported rocks, piled high until they created something that looked like a harbour wall. Boats carrying divers buzzed around — this is a tourist hotspot where they say the beaches are the very best in Brazil, which in Brazil is saying something. Its remoteness has given it added value, and metropolitan Brazilians view it as a fabled land.

I was drawn immediately to a shop, any shop, craving food that was not from a tin. I walked in the heat along an intermittent tarmac road that ran along the spine of the island and evaporated into a track, which then threaded its way through a collection of wooden housing. The colours of the paintwork were vivid, matching the richness of colour in the blooms and vegetation. People gave a friendly wave, dogs barked, children were curious, cars were few. I didn't seem to walk for long before I realised I had travelled half the length of this small island. The supermarket was dark and blissfully cool inside, lit by stark fluorescent tubes, and smelled deliciously of freshness. I sucked on an ice lolly. I could have grabbed a lettuce from the shelf there and then and ripped it apart and stuffed my mouth with it, so luscious did it look. Here I found sweet tomatoes, more cabbage, fresh bread and the dearest little saucepan I had ever seen, which I judged perfect for boiling eggs. For all these things I paid cruelly expensive prices — island prices.

Once back at the beach, I was drawn to a couple of tents set out by a wooden walkway that led from the harbour wall to the shore. In each tent was a two-ring gas burner, a pile of fish, and an enthusiastic woman with a broad grin who wanted nothing more than to cook for you. I sat down, took a cold drink, and saw others eating what looked like the most beguiling dishes the world had ever known. The menu meant nothing to me, so I got the woman's attention and pointed first to what someone else was eating, then back to me, and followed it up with a lot of nodding. She came back with a question I couldn't answer, then beckoned me to sit down. A while later, a plate laden with three freshly grilled fish arrived atop a mountain of salad and chips. My stomach, shrunk now by weeks of sparse feeding, groaned at the influx of so much food, but the appetite could not resist. I ate and ate, and could eat not another thing for a whole twenty-four hours after, and sat in the plastic chair by the beach with the satisfaction of an overfed python. And why not? I had made it to South America, almost.

In a shack by the shore sat the Authorities. I was dreading my first visit and took a seat on a row of plastic chairs, waiting my turn like a patient about to get a bad diagnosis. I felt sure there was some flaw in my paperwork and I would be deported. A young officer grabbed my passport and thumbed through it. He looked up. "What do you want to come here for? You could be back in London. Much better place." He spoke fine English, having spent five years living in Kilburn, and couldn't think of anywhere better in the world to be. There seemed little point in trying to persuade him that the island on which he worked, a UNESCO world heritage site, may have the edge on a north London suburb. It turned out that he was only on secondment here and spent much of his time trying to stem the tide of cross-border crime with Colombia on the far side of Brazil. I can see you might prefer Kilburn to that. I was then introduced to "a representative of the Navy", otherwise the harbour master. Very slowly he took a long list of every item of equipment on the boat. I had been in the hot little shack an hour and half before I won my release.

The lonely sail I had seen a couple of nights before finally caught up with me. It belonged to a fine wooden boat of a certain age called *Whanake*, and aboard were Chris and Suzanne. I was sitting in the cockpit as they rowed past on their way to the shore, and we greeted each other. We had both left from Cape Verde — they a few days ahead of me — but they had been imprisoned in the doldrums for longer than I had. Suzanne said she enjoyed the doldrums.

They were Pacific bound, setting off not only on the voyage of a lifetime but also to a new life in New Zealand, far from Scotland where their adventure had begun. They were filled with enthusiasm, had a clear and obvious love for each other and their boat, and nothing was going to draw a veil over their trip, not even the doldrums. Even more admirable was their essential simplicity of approach, often lost amongst cruising people in an age when all the comforts of shore are expected while afloat. There is now a generation of cruising people who know nothing other than running water in the galley, cockpit showers, furling headsails and electric anchor winches. Somehow, this had passed them by. A restricted budget helps. That evening they brought over huge slices of richly pink melon, which we sucked on and washed down with the dregs of a bottle of gin.

They told me they were not in any rush, provided they kept up with the changing seasons and took best advantage of them. Everything about them, from their boat to their way of thinking, was neat and shipshape. They didn't have money for marinas, and would seek anchorages wherever they could. They had stocked up with six months' worth of food and would not be falling into the expensive trap of island shopping, which had befallen me. Their only indulgence that day had been to buy themselves a huge tub of ice cream and spend the entire day on the beach devouring it. That's the way to do it. They'll remember that day for ever.

While my new friends spent another couple of days at anchor (over which they agonised greatly because this must be the most expensive anchorage in the world at almost £90 per day if there are two people on the boat), I decided to press on, mindful of getting to Brazil proper. So I bade them farewell, wished them luck, envied their ease more than a little, and set sail southwards towards the continent of South America. If I hesitated before leaving it was because the tip of the heavy Manson anchor had caught itself under a rock and I had to charge ahead at full speed, the engine screaming and the chain streaming behind me, in order to break free.

The distance to Salvador is about 500 miles and I always calculated on sailing a hundred miles a day, and more often than not found myself surprised to have done better. The brief encounter with land had been refreshing but left a sense that my real life was becoming less on land and more at sea. On that first night, I was pleased to be reunited with my old friends the stars and planets, and to resume the struggle to work out why Orion, an old friend at home and always best seen from my bathroom window on winter nights, was now upside down. The following morning dolphins played, coming briefly out of their own world and into mine, as my new friends on the island had. The ocean is a place of fleeting but intense acquaintance.

Two nights out and the going was gentle in a steady breeze out of the east. But perhaps I had been allowed too much ease. The harbinger of an hour of chaos was a sudden lurch, which had me up from my bunk in a split second. If there is one thing that you come to know as well as the beating of your own heart, it is the motion of the boat as she makes her way across the sea. Anything that disturbs that subtle rhythm is immediately felt, as insistent as the prick of a pin. Something is wrong, you know it, you feel it, because your boat has become a part of you, and for a sail to flap when it should not, or a rattle to appear where there should be silence, is as wounding as stubbing your own toe.

Something had happened. We were off course by almost 180 degrees and the wind was now from ahead; the boat had swung around of her own accord, out of control. At moments like these your mind races, seeking a reason. You look upwards at the flag at the masthead to see if the wind has shifted, then at the compass. You grab the wheel to get a feel of the steering and to dismiss morbid thoughts such as "the rudder has dropped off". Only when I finally looked over the stern did I discover the self-steering paddle was slapping from side to side, free to do as it wished — not in any kind of control. Either side of it hung two limp lengths of line and their chafed ends, all too clear in the light from my head torch.

I tried to decide how best to set the sails to keep us stable while I attempted a repair. I fumbled for a bag that contained bits of old line, took two pieces I thought would do the job, then had the tricky task of threading them down the tubes of the self-steering mount. This was like threading a needle while riding a galloping horse. As anyone who has threaded anything down a wide tube with only a narrow exit will know, it is one thing to start hopefully but another to arrive with an emerging rope at the other end. With a great deal of reaching over the stern, putting all my weight on my ribs (and cracking one in the process), I started to fish with my fingers for the rope's end, praying it would appear. I don't know how it was eventually achieved, probably more by chance than anything else, but just as I was on the point of giving up and resigning myself to endless hours on the helm, the cord appeared shyly at the far end of the tube, and with fingers outstretched I was able to grab it. The joy was overwhelming.

Land revealed itself as a distant smudge, as all continents do no matter how grand. They do not arrive in clouds of glory or on the song of trumpets, but as a smear hardly noticed at first but gradually forming into the unmistakable closeness of land. I didn't give a bugger. It was one of those bad-tempered days. The wind had fallen very light and I took the opportunity to refill the fuel tanks from the last of the spare I carried. I had been motoring through the night; the cabin was hot and stuffy from the heat of the engine, the noise drilling through my head, filling a space that had grown accustomed to the gentle sound of wind and waves. I hated that bloody engine and kicked an innocent cabin door for no good reason.

Then I had good reason for unease. The engine spluttered, then regained its composure but gave another stutter. This does not happen out of the blue. There must always be a reason. I guessed fuel contaminated with filth rising from the bottom of the tank after an uncomfortable patch of lumpy water. I switched it off before it took the decision for me, and resumed a very slow sail south.

Salvador was only a day away now. I gave up on the engine and planned accordingly. Needless to say, to add to the complexity of the situation it soon became clear that my landfall would come just as darkness had fallen. It was about eight in the evening and I had grabbed an early supper. The wind had come round till it was blowing from ahead. I bore away and we were making good speed towards a marker buoy around which I had to pass before heading north into the wide mouth of the Bay of All Saints, the large area of water in which sits Salvador on the eastern side. My navigation lights were still not working and so I had no means of making other ships aware of my presence. The batteries were low, and the electronic screen that showed my position was fading to greyness. I was now navigating on my wits.

It made for some of the best sailing since home. I leapt from cockpit to chart table, back to the wheel, back to chart, to and fro. I grabbed the binoculars and managed to recognise a red light, which I identified as being on the end of the harbour breakwater. I now had to let go of the wheel to prepare the anchor. I wondered, but didn't dare to hope, if the ailing engine would get me the last few yards into the anchorage. It spluttered half-heartedly into life, sounding as if it didn't really want to come out and play. All I needed was for it to take me a mere 50 yards in a direction it would have been difficult to sail. It coughed like an old man but it ran, and when I pushed the gear stick into ahead, it obliged.

Now I could let the anchor go. The boat settled back, the anchor bit. It was midnight. I saw the lights of high-rise blocks along the waterfront, as if I had sailed into a Manhattan skyline. But something was not quite right. I breathed the air yet felt nothing special. This was supposed to be a moment of triumph but I felt no emotion. Nor was there any great feeling of achievement, unlike my other landfalls, which lifted me to a new plane. Instead, there was a feeling of great unease. For the first time I wondered if I had made a great mistake in coming here.

I had yet to make up my mind about South America.

CHAPTER
TEN

BRAZIL — A NERVOUS TIME

My first thought on waking was to get the hell out of it. This is a city with a reputation for air that tastes of threat and reeks of the smell of violence. Yet Salvador is by no means the most violent city in Brazil, although it is trying hard to catch up. It manages a murder rate six times that of the United States, so it's made a good start. Vast areas of the city are given over to the infamous favelas — slums, really — ruled by gangs with guns to shoot and drugs to sell. Into this already toxic cocktail of violence you can add petty thieving, prostitution and kidnapping. Blacks are paid, on average, half of what whites earn, thus guaranteeing disorder. It was not the sort of place I wanted to be, and certainly nowhere I wanted to leave the boat, but it was time to return home once again, another leg completed, and there were no other options.

Even so, I thought the city looked half decent when seen through the early morning smog. For months I had wondered what it would look like, and how I would feel when it was spread out before me. The very fact of it being no longer an image in a pilot book made it an object of fascination.

I was anchored a little too close to a floating fuel barge, excusable in the darkness but I knew I would soon have to move. I lifted the anchor, drifted a little way to be clear, and dropped the hook again. Once settled, I attacked the oil filters and bled the air out of the fuel lines with workshop manual in hand — I am no gifted engineer but neither am I afraid of a spanner. My efforts gave the engine new life. I rewarded myself with a fried Spam breakfast.

I had found what I hoped would be a safe haven, somewhere I could leave the boat that was a step removed from the threatening atmosphere of downtown Salvador. I had read a recommendation of a place called Pier Salvador, and had made a booking. Bitter experience tells me that promises fall easy from the lips of the marine business but delivery happens with less certainty.

First impressions did not give confidence. The marina was built around the crumbling remains of a once dignified art-deco building, which had served in the 1930s as a boarding station for seaplanes working the islands in the outer bay. Its glory had faded, and substantially. Paint peeled, timber rotted, scruffy dogs barked. I moved at dead slow speed, wondering where the hell to go. Suddenly there were shouts from the shore and a small gang gathered, beckoning me towards them. I threw them lines which they caught and I was quickly secured before I had time to argue. A small, determined man with a bald head and glasses appeared. "I am Sandoval," he said in pidgin English. "I am owner." He was carrying a tray which bore a pint of chilled orange juice. This was perfect. I promised myself to beware of first impressions in Brazil.

In a crime-ridden city such as Salvador, where the streets are safe to walk only in places, where mugging and knife crime is as common as double parking in London, this little northern suburb of Salvador, called Ribiera, proved a perfect refuge. I never felt threatened here, and was always made welcome amongst the mostly black faces who beckoned me into their shops and ice cream parlours. If you were dropped here out of the blue, you would swear you were in Africa. Only the crumbling, Portuguese-style colonial architecture would suggest any land of European link. In fact, more African blood flows through the veins of this place than any other. Salvador was a main centre of the slave trade; thousands upon thousands of Africans would have been transported here on those benevolent trade winds only to be traded like cargo. Some stayed, clearly.

You can quickly turn native here; there's no point fighting it. You have to grab a can of beer like the rest of them, turn over the tomatoes lying in a box on the pavement if you want to find the best. Lacking in courage, I never made it into restaurants from which wafted addictive, spicy aromas, and never penetrated the throng of swarthy men who formed a ring around them; it was more than my cowardice would allow. I hated my lack of language.

Then I ventured into the big city. In what was to be the first in a series of long, hot rambles along lonely

102

docksides, I set off in search of Immigration, then Customs, and finally the Harbour Authority, which must be visited in strictly that order or the full force of bureaucratic anger would be felt. I saw myself slip easily behind the bars of one of those rat-infested South American jails that thriller writers are so keen on. I walked past desolate warehouses, flinching when I stepped into the shadows, bracing myself for the stab of the knife. I was seeking a tiny office where I could get my passport stamped. Then I would tramp another sweaty mile to the indifferent Customs office, where the processing of my papers was a grave intrusion into their cigarette time. Finally, a more relaxing visit to the Harbour Authority, which is a division of the Brazilian Navy and is protected by uniformed military wielding machine guns, so at least it felt safe to get my wallet out. Sandoval recommended I returned by bus because it was cheaper. He must be joking. I took a cab. You do not need to spend many hours in Brazil before you feel a crick in your neck from constantly looking over your shoulder.

I started to pack my things and prepare the boat for the following two months when I would be away. It was time to go home for Christmas. I thought these interruptions would be frustrating, but it all seemed to fit in with my wider plan to blend a little work with a little adventure, and I was more than ready to see the folks back home.

It rained heavily the day before I was scheduled to catch the plane. In my haste to get things shipshape, I slipped on the cabin steps and in trying to save myself

I suffered the painful sensation of a dislocated shoulder. It is a weakness of mine; I have done it twice before. I knew instantly what had happened and what the next painful hours would involve. To need a hospital in a city of which you know nothing, where you have not a word of the language and are in intense pain, is testing. Sandoval showed true depth of his kindness and took me to a local clinic where the doctor, in broken English, explained he was going to "fix me". I waited for the anaesthetic but none was offered. Instead he grabbed my throbbing arm and twisted. The pain had me reaching for the roof. In his half-decent English he told me, "We are going to fix this together", as if somehow I wasn't playing my part. At the first attempt he failed and I was now on the point of passing out. He then called his burly mate to apply more pressure on my now extended arm. Sandoval, who stayed with me like a true friend, could no longer watch. Two more attempts and with the pain now off the scale I breathlessly suggested we were making no progress. The doctor, if that's what he was, agreed. When I asked for some pain relief he told me, "I am sorry but we are not licensed for anaesthetic here." These are depressing words at times like this.

An hour later, after a mad car dash across this crazy town played out to the accompaniment of much hooting and shouting, I found myself in an accident hospital sitting alongside a row of lads who had come off their motorbikes and were covered in dripping wounds, grazes and vivid bruises. I was asked for £1,500. More pain. Five hours later I emerged with my shoulder back in place. Sandoval refused to allow me to return to the boat that night and instead I spent it at his smart home, sipping red wine by his pool. I was grateful for a clean and comfortable and roomy bed, and for being looked after as if I was his oldest friend.

Christmas back home was quickly done with and I have little memory of it. Libby said I wasn't really there, and that was true. It was a bit of a going-through-the-motions experience and all my thoughts were forward-looking now. For the next leg, I would have two crew. Mike, my brother-in-law, always bring his optimistic outlook to an adventure. He knows that sailing can drag you to the depths of despair but he always seems to emerge from it smiling. Our friend Alasdair has an intellectual air, but cooks well and is good company and is the only man I know who understands the mathematics of satellite navigation. Not a bad mix for a crew.

I had booked us into a bed and breakfast not a hundred yards from the boat. It looked good on the internet, but everything does. We arrived outside a corrugated garage door covered in vibrant graffiti, next to it a sinister and unlit hole in the wall which, we were told, led to our rooms for the night. It was late, the streets were deserted, dogs barked, the heavy thump of electric music played in the distance, it was very hot. It turned into a truly African experience. Around a small courtyard of beaten earth, from which grew unidenti-fied tropical trees, were rooms that looked like cells. Their windows were barred, each room lit by a single, bare bulb in the centre of the ceiling from which hung a slowly revolving fan. It was stiflingly hot, so even the dribble of the miserly cold shower was welcome. It was a mercy that we were too tired to worry about the cleanliness of the bed, or what might be breeding in the warm, moist atmosphere of the mattresses that had clearly seen many years' service. We went each to our cells like monks, bolted the doors and slept till breakfast. A very thin and elderly lady offered us food. "Bread?" she asked. We nodded. She put on her coat and made her way to the shop on the corner as slowly as her legs could carry her.

I stepped quickly along the marina pontoons and was overtaken with relief at seeing the boat again. It seems impossible that the boat you left in a different hemisphere will still be there when you return; that the milk carton you forgot to throw away will be on the galley top precisely where you left it; that a coil of rope would be hanging from the cleat in exactly the same way it was months before. So much around us changes, yet something 5,000 miles away is preserved as if in aspic. The crew was anxious to be off, as all crews are. I walked what was now a familiar path through the commercial district of downtown Salvador, once again down the full length of those threatening quaysides, avoiding eye contact, always glancing over my shoulder, never allowing myself to be alone down any street or alley. We planned an escape that night. As we waited for the tide, dusk fell and with it came a fleet of small, open boats, casting nets to catch fish. The water was now high enough for us to get over the shallow spit that protected the bay, and just before the hour I fired up the engine. While it warmed up I thought I might pump the bilge. And so my troubles began.

It was soon clear that it was not water I was pumping from the inside of the boat. The air was filled with the unmistakable sickly scent of diesel; the gush from the pump had a pinkish colour and the surface of the water around started to shimmer as a thin film of oil spread like a plague. It could only have come from one place — the bilge was full of diesel. I checked the level of fuel in the tank and found it nearly empty, and recalled that when I left two months before, it was full to the brim. I shrugged it off as a minor problem. Big mistake. I should have cut the engine and stayed put, but with the desire for adventure almost overwhelming I decided to press on and get away from Salvador. Impatience can be cruising's greatest enemy.

Uneasily, we made our way across the vast Bay of All Saints, heading for a small harbour on the north side of the island of Itaparica. We had not gone far before the engine faltered, coughed, spluttered and almost died. Like a man who refuses to give up the last gasp of life, it struggled on till I put it out of its misery with the stop button. Now began the first of many fanciful discussions as to what could be the fault. Where was the leak, how might we fix it? Here the crew divided. Mike, a solid sort of a guy who will rise to any emergency, distanced himself from intellectual argument surrounding fuel filters and instead entertained us with headlines from the *Daily Telegraph*, which, by some miracle, were being flashed daily to his Kindle. Alasdair, a software author and mathematician, naturally brought his ingenious mind to the task in hand. Whereas my first instinct is always to reach for a tool and start undoing things, he preferred a discursive analysis before proceeding. And so it went on with all possible outcomes discussed, all remedies assessed, no solution arrived at.

That night at anchor proved to be a restless one. Music blared from a shoreside restaurant with an intensity that would have shaken the rivets from a warship. It was raucous, thumping, hissing, cutting-through-the-air music. It hammered at the boat, into our heads and deep into our minds till the early hours when dawn finally quietened it. I lay in my bunk. I was hot, and the thin sheet that covered me was soaked with perspiration. I wished as hard as I could that I was anywhere but this place. Somewhere cool and quiet would do, like Shetland.

Despite the first cup of tea the following morning, I was filled with an overwhelming sense that heading further south might not be the thing to do. The boat felt a little broken, I too felt like damaged goods with a shoulder that functioned but had no strength and was in danger of a repeated, painful, expensive and inconvenient dislocation. It all seemed too much to handle, and as the sweat dribbled down my face and depression took hold, I told the lads that I was planning on going no further than Rio, and that would be the end of the voyage. They took it well. Life went on. Mike gave us more cheery readings from the *Daily Telegraph*, Alasdair discovered that in the overnight heat all the pears had turned to mush. Then, quietly and reflectively and trying hard not to show our disappointment, we lifted the anchor and at very slow and spluttering ahead we crept the 10 miles back to Pier Salvador where I commenced, once again, the round of offices — Immigration, Customs and Harbour Authority — informing them that we had not left as planned, but had returned. My feet were now covered in blisters.

To hell with it; this voyage was now over. Even Rio was too far. We would make the best of where we were and explore the harbours and rivers around the bay and enjoy an intensive time of creek-crawling, and sod the ocean. And sod Rio. And sod all points south. To their credit, the crew agreed. And sod the diesel too, they added. We'd sail and reserve the engine for light work. That decided, life became more relaxed.

We shopped. Sandoval advised that we took a taxi to a large supermarket and back again for safety — it was not in a good part of town. Somewhere in that supermarket I managed to lose my credit card. In one of the most crime-ridden cities in the world, I had lost my grip on the most precious bit of plastic in my present life. I blamed those damned money belts I felt forced to wear; a sweaty crotch is no place to have to dive into when you need some cash and I did it with great impatience. In doing so, the credit card must have slipped out. Alasdair suggested I asked the armed guard if it had been handed in. I gave a long and hollow laugh and told him I wasn't going to waste my time. Alasdair was more determined and returned with a broad grin on his face to tell me it *had* been handed in. It crossed my mind that although this is a famously thieving society, I could not have been certain of such an honest outcome back home.

Ever glad to see a bargain, especially in the booze department, Mike and I bought copious amounts of cheap red wine at less than a quid a bottle — what value! It was labelled with a holy picture of a saint, a bit like the once-familiar old Blue Nun labels, but no alarm bells rang. Imagine our disappointment when it turned out to be sweet, sickly, undrinkable communion wine, sold in supermarkets here next to the rows of tropical spirits. It was not the sort of communion we wanted and it followed the diesel overboard.

We ate a muted lunch. Alasdair broke the silence. "You've come all this way. You'll never forgive yourself if you don't go on now." Without hesitation, and to my surprise, I instantly agreed. Someone had to say it. He had taken the initiative and I will be forever grateful to him. We *would* head south. Back to plan A.

In the depths of the night we moved into a large and plush marina in Salvador, the one nearest the sea. This had none of the homeliness of Pier Salvador. We were now in a land of motor boats staffed by twenty-first-century slaves. Where labour is cheap, where jobs are scarce, where there is no support from any kind of social security if you do not have a job, every boat had a (black) boy who polished it end to end, then washed it down, then polished it again, and did this every day if the boat was used or not. I was told the pay was pitiful. Salvador's slavery days are not quite over.

We found a supermarket and stocked up for several hundred miles. Alasdair decided to hunt for a post office to send a postcard home — an email would not do. He wandered off into the back streets with the innocence of a trusting child strolling into a lion's cage. Dressed like an English gentleman abroad with his Tilley hat and Bermuda shorts, he might as well have carried a "Come and Mug Me" sign. We doubted we would ever see him again. Mike remarked, only half-joking, "We'll give him an hour and then start ringing round the hospitals." Brazil is such hard work.

We sailed with a fair breeze, eating up the five hundred or so miles south. The wind varied in strength from very little to something of a blow for a short period around five o'clock every evening; this became part of the pattern of daily life. We were still burdened with irritations, not least the diesel problem, which still haunted us, and also the failing batteries. I should have had them replaced in Salvador, but in a country where every task presents itself as an insuperable difficulty it was simply a job too far. As they were not completely dead, I took the wishful option and thought they might, somehow, sort themselves out. Ships bound for the vast port of Santos became more frequent and there were times when their navigation lights could be seen on all sides of us. All I could show was my forward-looking steaming light, aided by a powerful torch if anything came up astern of us. Distant lightning sparked inland, unheard and therefore many miles away, and the storms never made it out to sea.

Towards the end of five days of gentle, fair-wind rolling over blue and crested seas, a distinct loom could be seen over the starboard bow which could only be the distant lights of Rio de Janeiro. How exotic. But before then, and in order to break the journey, I offered the crew a choice of two anchorages. The first was off a fishing harbour close by a cement works. The other was at the flash resort of Buzios, where the rich and lovely hang out and where Brigitte Bardot chose to hide back in the 1960s with her then Brazilian boyfriend, thus ensuring a small fishing town would soon come to rival St Tropez as a celebrity magnet. Jagger and Madonna are now regulars here. Bardot worship continues. There is a statue of her, a boulevard carries her name, and there's even a plaque to mark the spot where she and the boyfriend hung out. I told my crew all this while stressing that the anchorage off the cement works was still on offer. Strangely, they chose to cuddle up with the spirit of Bardot; I would have gone for the chemical works option, having had enough of the thumping sounds of Brazil and the acres of flesh that parade the streets of these rich little resorts. Beach wear is so skimpy here that there's hardly enough of it to wipe a dipstick.

Having agreed to Buzios for the night, I announced that there was a price to pay: we would tackle the diesel problem once and for all and only then go ashore. Their private thoughts on this matter were not shared. At some point during these amateur and often hilarious attempts at marine engineering, I asked Mike to blow hard down the fuel pipe in case there was a blockage.

He blew, cheeks bursting, with the force of a state trumpeter at a Coronation. Then I heard a noise. I asked him to stop. Do it again! I bent my ear towards the galley. Again! I could hear a hiss, like leaking gas, every time he blew. Entirely by accident we had found our problem. A hole in the copper fuel pipe. We'd really found it! No amount of reasoning or analysis could ever have led us to this. Archimedes could not have been more thrilled at such a fundamental discovery. It explained everything. It was the reason the tank had emptied into the bilge back in Salvador, it was the reason the engine was sucking air and faltering. This was the needle-sized hole in a haystack of pipework and we had found it.

Alasdair applied his mind to the repair but I already had spanners in hand before so much as a constructive thought had formed in his beautiful mind. "Careful," he warned me as I applied grips to pipe. I ignored him. It was soon removed, a dab of epoxy glue was applied to the spot so small that you needed your glasses to see it, then the whole lot was put back and the tedious procedure was undertaken to rid the fuel lines of air, otherwise the engine would not fire. We sweated and cursed and laughed while the rich and self-regarding paraded themselves along the Buzios waterfront. That night we would be the only males in town wearing hydrocarbons for aftershave.

I was already feeling overdosed at the sight of mountains of Brazilian bare flesh, but it was Rio that delivered the full aversion therapy. The day started well after a night at sea. The granite mass of the Sugarloaf

Mountain materialised in the dawn, the mist lifting to slowly reveal the outline of the fabled city of Rio de Janeiro. Christ the Redeemer himself spread his arms in greeting from atop a neighbouring hill. Everything spoke of welcome.

It was breakfast time when we came alongside in Marina Gloria, the only marina on Rio's waterfront. I had been told to look out for floating sewage and invading rats but we saw neither, although other vermin were to catch up with us later. Let's be clear about that famous Copacabana Beach, which was close. The cruel truth, which all potential visitors should know, is that it is nothing more than a narrow strip of hot sand fringing a rather grubby stretch of water. On the landward side is a four-lane highway and this fronts five unbroken miles of high-rise hotels. The beach is lit at night to the intensity of the perimeter wire of a high-security prison to frighten off the muggers. Tourists travel half the world to wobble their fat arses to the incessant beat of the music here. Every hole into which a loudspeaker can be fitted has been so equipped. I wonder they don't have them up their backsides. At the far end of the beach is the suburb of Ipanema from where the girl who is "tall and tan and young and lovely" comes from. I've no doubt she's gorgeous, but the effort of seeing for myself was just too much. The lads walked on, I went back to the boat. I noticed one thing as I strolled: anyone, even of modest wealth, lived in a gated community patrolled by armed guards and all apartment blocks had barred windows even to the fourth floor. The result is that it is the people who have nothing who have all the freedom, while those with possessions are the prisoners. A topsy-turvy place.

Expecting that a walk by the cathedral on a quiet Sunday morning might be a safe thing to do, we were professionally and gracefully mugged the next morning. It was so neatly done that it was almost admirable in its execution, and clearly well practised. As we strolled, we sensed three lads creeping up behind us. We quickened our pace only for three more to emerge from the shadows in front to bring us to a halt. A blade appeared and then much urgent shouting of "Money! Money! Money!" How they knew we were British I wasn't certain but perhaps Alasdair's Tilley hat was the giveaway. Mike lost a camera, me a few quid, Alasdair his glasses and a bit of cash. He seemed quite upset about it but I was less bothered. It was just another tourist tax. As long as you give them what they ask for they are very unlikely to do you any harm. Just as they were in the act of going through our pockets, a bus drew up and the passengers stared in horror at what they were seeing, but none came forward to help. It's part of daily life.

Alasdair, still angry by the time made it back to the boat, went to report the mugging to the tourist police. He was met with a shrug. "We get mugged too!" he was told. The same day, the crew of a neighbouring French boat were mugged just a few steps outside the marina perimeter. In something of a rage at this lawless and suffocating place, I declared in a voice loud enough for the Redeemer on his hilltop to hear, "I *don't* want to be here. I want to go to Patagonia and *Brazil is in the fucking way!*" And that was the truth.

I gave Brazil one last chance. About 60 miles west of Rio, the Bahía Isla Grande is a vast bay of islands set amidst sheltered waters with safe anchorages. If you are beyond rich, this is yet another place to build your dream shore-side house. The only hint that this paradise is not perfect might be an armed guard patrolling the grounds of your unoccupied mansion, or a (black) lad sweeping your private beach for the umpteenth time that day, even though no one has set foot on it. That's the sort of place Isla Grande is.

Tucked away in corner of the bay is the town of Paraty — the Venice of Brazil. It sits in a landscape of tropical forest, high mountains and tumbling waterfalls. The skies are wild here and quickly changing: black and threatening one minute, vivid blue the next. Downpours are regular and truly torrential. The streets are cobbled, and horses and carts replace cars and delivery vans (except on Wednesdays). They call it Venice because the main thoroughfares flood to at least ankle height every spring tide.

We said goodbye to Alasdair here, who braved the 200-mile bus ride to Rio alone, and as Mike and I left for the next leg 400 miles south I had a sense that I was at last "getting there", and fell into a more concentrated but relaxed cruising frame of mind. The playgrounds were behind us and more workmanlike sailing lay ahead. We had two days of torrential rain compensated for by a following wind; it was rain like I have never felt it before and it cascaded down the sails in torrents, drumming on the deck, rattling down the scuppers. It was refreshing after the sultry heat of the enclosed and windless Bahía Isla Grande, and it came with a promise that no matter how wet we might be, as soon as the sun came out we would be dry again within a few minutes. There was freshness in the atmosphere now. We were 24 degrees south of the equator and I was leaving both the tropics behind and the discomforts of Brazil. I was glad to be rid of them both.

We enjoyed what I would call a proper twilight for the first time for 3,000 miles since north of the Cape Verde islands. It was a languid sinking into the blackness of night rather than the switching off of the sun that happens in the tropics. My mind felt sharper now it was spending less time under the grill of the equatorial sun.

It was now the end of February and another chapter in the voyage was coming to an end. I would soon have to return home again, this time for six whole months. I was becoming used to these interruptions and didn't mind them. They were mostly to my advantage; with the southern summer coming to an end it was as well that I would be at home and working while the winter down there blew itself out. With a sigh of relief, Mike dropped the Brazilian courtesy flag that had been flowing from the mast for 3,000 miles now, and replaced it with the Uruguayan one, which bore an optimistic image of a benevolent sun.

Now we must face the River Plate, a vast swathe of water 200 miles wide at its mouth, making it the widest river in the world. Some say it should properly be described as a gulf. On its northern shore is Uruguay, the second smallest country in South America, with its capital Montevideo. On the opposite bank stands Buenos Aires, the capital of Argentina. It is largely a shallow bit of water, not unlike our own Thames estuary. Short but very sharp storms breed here and a change in the weather can be as abrupt as the throwing of a switch from calm to gale. Seabirds became more frequent, I noticed.

With our intended harbour of Piriapolis almost in sight, and a plate of South American steak much on our minds, inevitably the wind drew ahead and strengthened, rapidly building and bringing driving rain. It never does to think you have it in the bag.

The wind rose to an angry 30 knots, and the engine was little help as the seas were short and stopped the boat dead in the water, as such waves always do. A fierce current appeared out of nowhere, running hard against us and we made no progress. For two hours we flogged on, resigned to another night of dreary onboard rations. That succulent steak began to vanish like a desert mirage. Then, as quickly as the wind had arrived, it departed. We were left in a flat calm. By teatime we were alongside the concrete harbour wall of *Wild Song*'s new home, and no steak ever tasted sweeter.

CHAPTER
ELEVEN

URUGUAY — DEEPER INTO THE SOUTH ATLANTIC

Uruguay was damp, chilly and in partial hibernation when I returned in September at what should be the start of the southern spring, although I found little evidence of it. *Wild Song* sat lifeless, all the spirit drained from her, propped on all sides by heavy baulks of timber in the boatyard beside the harbour at Piriapolis. Dwarfed by rough, tough yachts around her, she looked like a nervous puppy amidst bigger, barking dogs. These deeply serious yachts, built of sturdy steel or aluminium, dwarfed her on all sides; she was like a rowing boat amongst the warships. These were the big boys round here, earning their living taking lucrative charter parties to Antarctica and coming to Piriapolis every winter for refurbishment and to take advantage of the more lenient bureaucracy. All bore the scars of serious skirmishes with wind, wave, weather and ice: the kind of damage that sailing at high latitudes inflicts on all boats, whatever their size. No wonder *Wild Song* looked small, almost pocket-sized amongst them. Did she seem to be trembling a little at the thought of what might lie ahead? Did she know she would be the smallest boat heading south from Uruguay that season? Enough to send a shiver down my already chilly spine.

Piriapolis is a small family resort which in Britain you would describe as a candy-floss and fish-and-chips kind of a place. It is set around a sandy bay and backed by wooded hills that give way to blue, misty mountains in the distance, atop one of which stands a large cross. It is an easy place to be fond of. It was also a place of significance in terms of this voyage, for from here on there could be no going back, not for me. This really was a point of no return. Once I had set off south I was committed to going all the distance to the deep south, to the Beagle Channel and then Cape Horn — to the very edge of the world. There are harbours in Argentina, of course, any of which could seduce me to change my mind. But once I had left the River Plate then shelter would become less certain and the ports increasingly less attractive as the weather becomes ever more bad-tempered. None are places to linger. Thoughts of giving up had already crossed my mind back in Rio and I wasn't prepared for that torment all over again. We were heading south, me and my little ship, and that was decided.

I walked the cold, wet and windy streets of this deserted resort, totally unprepared for the new face it was showing. Back in February it had been heat and hustle; families slurping ice cream, beach bars pouring cold beers, the Uruguayan Ladies Beach Volleyball Championships about to take place, and every evening the town was smothered in the scent of wood smoke and burnt meat which poured from the barbecues and grills that were the central features of the larger restaurants.

But not in September. Hardly a cafe was open; the few people on the streets were huddled under thick layers, the seafront shops were boarded up, the barbecues were cold and replaced by a couple of puny logs burning in an open grate, giving a paltry heat. In a place like Uruguay, where the summers are hot and steamy and winters brief but chilly, heating has to be laid on but is clearly not taken seriously. The houses, they tell me, are not built with insulation. So, for the weeks when temperatures drop, the people suffer and it shows on their faces. I found it a perplexing climate: cold one day, hot the next, then back to cold. A jumper-on, jumper-off kind of place. And another thing — at noon the sun is noticeably to the north of you. I was still not used to it.

I spent three weeks preparing the boat; taking her apart bit by bit and putting her back together again, replacing varnish that had peeled, remembering the mechanical irritations of the passage so far and trying to rid the boat of them. Not even the simple task of getting a boat ready for sea is easy in South America. I was in desperate need of new batteries, which had caused me hours of fretting ever since way back in the Canaries. I was strongly warned to avoid ones made in Argentina or Brazil — they would certainly be of poor quality. I should search instead for imported ones from the USA or Europe, and expect to pay a premium price. I had enlisted the help of an amiable Irishman,

Laurence, and his girlfriend, Elisa, who together run a boat caretaking service, largely for English-speaking boat owners, which is very convenient. They started the search for batteries on my behalf, not knowing it was to be a hunt that was to take on the proportions of that for the Holy Grail. The first dealer said there were good batteries on a ship coming from America and arriving on Sunday, but his ship never came in. He said he meant the following Sunday, but nothing happened then either. Another had batteries in stock . . . no, hang on a minute, they were starter batteries. And so it went on. In the meantime, I turned to the local chandler for some rope but he shrugged and said he didn't have any. "Come back in six weeks' time when I have some money to buy some," he said.

I spent days waiting for things to happen. They rarely did. I often walked the streets to clear my head after so much time spent upside down servicing the engine, or peering into the bilge, or stopping the sink from dripping. I got used to the crisscross layout of the town, and became familiar with the hardware shops and what they stocked so that I could cobble together anything I needed. I was soon on nodding terms with the ladies in the bakery and the laundry, and after regular evening visits I was even able to raise a smile on the face of the woman who guarded the showers and whose sole job it was to make sure you paid. She never looked happy in her work or, I imagined, in her life either. She had a face that I guessed had not cracked a smile in many a year and had forgotten how to.

I remember most vividly the deep friendliness of the place where my poor attempts at Spanish did not return blank stares or looks of irritation, as they might in other places, but instead laughter and helpfulness. These were good people and they supported me at every turn. If I have a regret — and it is a deficiency in the very nature of yacht cruising wherever you are in the world — it is that I didn't get to know them even better. The boat demanded so much attention that I have no idea where the hours and minutes went. Three weeks seems such a long period to achieve something so minor as a small boat ready to go to sea, but that was how long it took. And just as I thought everything was ready and I could relax, when the tanks had been filled, the cabin floor swept, the winches greased and such trivial things as the cabin cushions plumped, nature took the opportunity to remind me exactly where I was, and give me a taste of what the future might hold.

It was a Thursday morning at the end of my third week of fitting-out and my new crew, another Chris, was due to arrive in three days. It was not an especially windy morning, a bit breezy but no more than that, but I had been tricked into a false sense of security, for the arm of the marina in which I was moored was so well protected by a hillside that a hurricane could blow from the east and you would not know. Which was, unbeknown to me, precisely what was happening.

By mid-morning the wind had risen a little but nothing to cause any anxiety. In fact, I don't think I noticed it at all. Then came a gust that caught my attention, then another but a little sharper, and out of curiosity I switched on the instruments. It was blowing just above 20 knots — nothing special about that. Then, just as my head was deep in a job, there was a low thud like a punch from a boxing glove, as if we had been hit by an immense force. The boat heeled to the blow as if this malevolent giant's hand had taken hold of her and was trying to push her hard over, deep into the water. The wind blew hard now with a scream like that of an angry ghost. I leapt up and saw the wind speed was now 37 knots — gale force and noteworthy.

Five minutes later it was nudging 40 knots, then 45 in the gusts. It peaked at 51. What had once been the placid waters of a large and safe harbour had become a boiling cauldron and a treacherous spot. Big yachts felt the force too, heeling to the gale like daisies to the breeze. The first of many big waves piled over the harbour wall, crashing on to fishing boats moored in what was usually complete shelter. Then the second came, larger and heavier, carrying a serious weight of water, enough to sink small craft. As soon as I'd checked my own lines and made sure that all was secure, I sat in the cockpit and simply stared at the scene, mesmerised by the sudden and violent change that had taken place. Weather is supposed to change slowly, surely and steadily, at least that was my northern-hemisphere understanding of it. This was a new world of weather I found myself in.

I felt a vibration thrum through the boat, which over a minute firmed up into a regular rattle. When it had reached the pitch of machine-gun fire I put on full oilskins and went on deck to investigate. The wind had caught part of the headsail, the yankee, and was toying with it like a kitten with a ball of wool. Slowly it started to unwind, cracking now in the wind that was nudging force ten. There was no possibility of winding it back. A passing sailor leapt aboard to help me but two of us could make no progress against the storm. "Get more lines out!" he urged me in broken English. "How long will this last?" I asked. "It could be two days," he shouted back.

I looked at the lines which had once seemed so strong but were now stretched way beyond their normal length and looked ready to part. I put out extra, and just in time because the waters were rising and the concrete walkway to which I was moored was soon awash, with the rubbish bins floating away and the electricity sockets fizzing and popping before blowing their fuses. Even in the confines of one of the safest harbours for scores of miles, I would not be able to get ashore till this storm had passed. So I sat and watched my faithful and vital headsail slowly disintegrate before my eyes. Within minutes it was in tatters, with only remnants clinging to the forestay and detached bits of cloth draped like bedraggled Christmas streamers around the rigging of the boat downwind of me. The sail was now useless, but the vibration of its flogging was still rattling the mast and rigging, and that worried me.

I could have resigned myself to the shock of it all and spent the day frozen to the cockpit seat, but with a little considered thought and ingenuity — which had totally escaped me in the heat of the moment — clutching a rope, I crept along the deck on hands and knees for safety. After an immense struggle I managed to get a couple of full turns round the forestay and back to a winch on the mast. I started to wind. The rattle and the shaking and the disintegration slowly came to an end. The stable door was shut but the horse was long gone. The damage had been done. In a place where three weeks of effort had so far failed to produce a hint of a battery, what chance of a complex sail repair?

By late afternoon I was beginning to hate the noise of the wind. It became a constant, exhausting nag, never letting up. It had ceased to be a whistle and became a continuous roar, as if a low-flying jet was circling overhead. It made me short-tempered, and probably a little scared. It did not escape me that in the southernmost parts of this continent, 40 knots of wind was almost commonplace. The instruments now showed a full force ten. For six hours the wind never cut me any slack and worked at everything. Like a misbehaving child, it got its fingers into everything, determined to break whatever came its way.

Then it was gone, in an instant, as if it had tried too hard and had blown its own fuse. By seven that night, a child could have rowed a dinghy across the harbour. By bedtime it was almost forgotten. But not the tatters of the headsail now hanging limp in a gentle breeze that were as mocking as the storm had been. In reminding me of the treacherous waters into which I was about to sail, it had done me no harm; yet in undoing a chunk of work I had laboured over for the previous three weeks,

126

it had done me no favours. And still the batteries were nowhere to be seen.

But another thought was now pressing, and one that had been with me for a large part of the voyage so far. The question was — where would it end? I like to have an inkling of the future; it is a fault of mine. I am always reaching for the next thing before the one in hand is complete but, unusually for me, I could see no clear outcome to this voyage. I had no idea in which direction my reach would take me.

There were several options but the one marked "aimless drifting" was never on my agenda. It is all too easy to sail on for ever, as many cruising people do, dropping anchor where they will for as long as they wish; but I had a family, a job, and a living to earn and, anyway, I did not want to be an ocean drifter. I have never met one I thought was truly happy. They speak with enthusiasm of their freedoms, and it is easy to envy their casual approach to timetables and plans that most of us are obliged to adhere to. Yet only in a few cases have I sensed true satisfaction, and that was always amongst those who had some kind of goal, even if no deadline. The ones who hung around in harbours for months on end, preparing for voyages they were never going to make, seemed like people who were waiting for a bus that was never going to come to take them to a place that never existed. We are built to have aims and ambitions, and without them how do we know which way to steer ourselves? I understood this, and believed it, and so this crossroads of a place was as good a spot as any to make up my mind as to exactly where I was going.

In my grand plan, constructed from the comfort of an armchair back home, I would sail round the tip of South America, head into the Pacific Ocean, then strike out into the vastness of that stretch of water in search of . . . And here was the problem. What exactly was I searching for? I had already mentioned one idea. It was to voyage to a small island, Nomwin Atoll, part of Micronesia, on the far side of the Pacific to the north of Australia. It was the tiny coral island on which Nicholas had landed when aboard the tall ship *Europa*, and about which he wrote with such sincere affection and clarity of observation. I always felt it was on that island that he really grew up, not in years but in perceptions and understandings. So that was my plan: to sail there in his wake, hoping a little of what inspired him would provide some satisfaction for me.

But in the long night watches in the tropics I had already begun to have my doubts that a pilgrimage would offer anything. From a practical point of view, the distances across the Pacific are huge, measured in tens of thousands of miles. I had already done six thousand by the time I started to think all this through and that was beginning to feel like plenty. Nor did the thought of yet more tropical islands appeal to me, to be honest. For me, a white sandy beach with a palm-tree fringe yields enough satisfaction for an afternoon, but no longer. Mountains and pastures are more my inspiration. Anyway, I did not want to be away from home for the several years it would take to sail to

Nomwin and back again. It would be a pointless exercise.

This was a voyage during which I wanted to achieve a deeper understanding of Nicholas by peeling back the layers of his writing to see if there was something that had so far escaped me. I didn't need long tropical passages to achieve that. All that was necessary was to have space and peace in which to apply the mind, in particular to the "Silence at the Song's End" poem. To sail to Nomwin would be an act of sentimental tourism so I struck it off the agenda, and the instant I did so I realised it was the right thing to do.

Instead I devised a new voyage that would fill me with the same thrill of discovery that Nicholas had experienced, and it was conveniently to hand. I needed to go no further than the place famously called the "uttermost end of the Earth".

It might be there that I would hear the silence at the song's end, with its promise of a world to come.

CHAPTER
TWELVE

TOWARDS THE
ROARING FORTIES

Leaving any harbour, especially one of which you have grown fond, is always hard. It calls for no small amount of pluck. No matter how many times you have done it, whether you are aiming high, as I was, or merely voyaging from one side of your pond to another, leaving is still an effort. Why go anyway? What is better about "there" that is missing in "here"?

The sea off Piriapolis was lumpy, choppy and reminiscent of the grey North Sea. Like all shallow estuaries, the sea has a spiky feel to it and the waves are not at all like the gentle roll of the ocean's curls. The Plate was brown and soupy after the stirring by the storm and the breeze had infuriatingly dropped to a gentle whisper with hardly the strength to fill the sails, leaving us in that maddening state of slopping from side to side, bouncing from wave to wave, chop to chop, but making little forward progress. But a breeze came, as it always does, and the engine was stilled as the night sky cleared and we set a course for Mar del Plata in Argentina, 200 miles to the south.

Chris, my new crew, was settling in. He had plenty of home waters experience and was seeking to broaden his horizons. It is difficult to sail with people you do not know and with whom you have only had a brief acquaintance, but he had a quick mastery of the sails, the reefing gear and eventually the self-steering. I have sympathy, as the Monitor wind vane steering can look like something a maniac has made out of Meccano. I have sat for hours observing the way its wind vane drives a gear, which shifts a cog, which moves a blade, which drags a line, which brings the boat back on your intended course; all without electricity, electronics or processors. This is elemental engineering, with wind to drive the boat, wind to steer her, wind to keep her on course. You are sapping the breeze of everything it has yet it is exploitation of the best possible kind. From the sceptical look on his face, I think Chris preferred the electrics on his boat back home and the certainties that pushing a button can (sometimes) give you.

It was the best possible start I could have hoped for. In a strengthening breeze and across an ever flatter sea, *Wild Song* sailed as vigorously as I have ever known, making no fuss about it and certainly not throwing any water across the decks. It was just steady, untroubled progress. I was in no rush and had no desire to go any faster. The next morning, in a following wind, I started to hoist the Parasailor, that large blue and white sail similar to a spinnaker but built more like a parachute with acres of light, floating cloth. There remains something theatrical about the hoisting of it — a kind of will it/won't it? — and the hoist didn't go well. One line was clipped the wrong side of the forestay, and the downhaul, which pulls a thin, nylon sock over the whole sail when you want to dowse it, didn't look quite right. I was nervous, anyway. Winds here can come from any direction at any strength. On the one hand I wanted to show off this beautiful sail to Chris; on the other I knew I might be setting myself up for trouble. I dropped it to the deck, stuffed it in its bag, and suggested we waited for another day. An extra knot of speed at this stage was not worth the worry.

Mar del Plata loomed over the horizon at dawn like a poor man's Manhattan, its high-rise blocks running for mile after mile along this featureless coast. When the Argentinians have as many millions of empty acres as they do, and when they have a stunning and varied coastline which stretches for over a thousand miles, why they choose to spend their holidays living on top of each other defeats me.

"Identify yourself!" a voice crackled on the radio, insistent but courteous. It is a fault of radio operators that they have no understanding that on a small boat you might have things to do other than talk to them, and at that moment we were concentrating hard on getting into the harbour in one piece. Across the harbour mouth, between the two pier heads, was white, breaking water — a certain sign of a shallow bank of sand or shingle just beneath the surface. To hit the ground in such a place is to risk grave damage to a boat. "Identify yourself!" he repeated. Impatiently I gave him the boat's name but that was not sufficient. He wanted call sign, nationality, number of crew, last

132

port, destination, colour of socks ... Welcome to Argentina.

I suggested we edged towards the white water to take a closer look, with Chris urging me (correctly) further to the east. Then, in an instant, before there was any time to change our minds, the white water was not ahead of us but all around us, lifting us up and dropping us into a bubbling cauldron and then, out of nowhere, a great lump of it reared up and with a great shove we slewed sideways into the flat water of the harbour. Catching our breath, we turned right through a little swing bridge into an inner harbour packed with boats, all belonging to members of the Yacht Club Argentino, where we were to be guests.

One boat caught my eye. It was the cream-hulled *Whanake*, last seen 2,000 miles ago in Fernando de Noronha, the tropical island off the north coast of Brazil. Chris and Suzanne had stayed in my mind, and I had thought of them often. It had been their relaxed style of cruising, and their untroubled approach to it, that I had found so beguiling; just selling up and sailing off. They were not hurrying, but extracting all that was to be had from every mile of their journey, which was weighed down neither with money nor timetable. I wondered if the magic would survive over the many, many miles that lay ahead of them as they headed for a new home in New Zealand.

Over coffee I learned that their boat had wintered well in Uruguay, and so had they, and their enthusiasm was undimmed. But they too were apprehensive of the Roaring Forties ahead.

133

"It's good to have someone to talk to who isn't Chris!" Suzanne remarked as we sat around their cabin table eating Irish stew as the yellow flames of their oil lamps glistened on the deep brown varnished wood around us. We compared notes and agreed on a loud cheer at finally leaving Brazil behind, and both of us had lumps in our throats at saying farewell to Uruguay. "I knew we'd bump into you somewhere or other," said Suzanne, mending my frayed and tattered burgee with her sewing machine. "It's time to do some real sailing," muttered Chris. "It seems like I've done nothing for years but row ashore to go shopping in some run-down Spanish-speaking town or other."

Here we had our first skirmish with the Argentine authorities. It was a typical pointless, time-wasting and expensive encounter and was a foretaste of things to come. The marina manager said we would need Health Clearance. A short while later, an elderly lady walked towards us dressed, somewhat theatrically, in a white doctor's coat. Was she about to snap on rubber gloves and examine us? We sat on a convenient bench. In her broken English and my fractured Spanish the conversation turned to diseases. Did we have any? Chris and I agreed we had none. "Good," she said, and duly signed our health certificate. That was it. Except she now wanted thirty quid in exchange for this ridiculous document. You have to keep smiling, it's the only way.

She asked where we were heading, and although it was none of her business and I didn't really have time to sit and chat, I had learned that a little civility goes a long way. I told her we were almost certainly bound for Ushuaia in the Beagle Channel, and her eyes moistened. "Ah," she said. "My beloved grandson. He is in Ushuaia! He teaches snowboarding." Many pictures were now dragged from the depths of her handbag as supporting evidence, each with a lengthy story told in quick-fire Spanish which left me nodding but not understanding much. It was tedious, but painless, and she quickly signed us off and welcomed us to Argentina. Always say something nice about the grandson is the moral of that encounter.

The experience of a "new beginning" was a recurring one, and it felt as if the big adventure would always begin at the next harbour, not at this one. This time, though, the departure from Mar del Plata felt different. I was sailing into waters of which I had no experience nor any real understanding. For a start, I had no real grasp of how the weather worked down here. Back home we know the consequence of a falling barometer and a dark sky to windward — bad weather. Here it was the opposite: a rising barometer and a clearing sky were the things of which one should be seriously afraid, for this is when the ferocious cold fronts come and beat you up in a damaging way. So much to learn and cope with. All my instincts learned over years were becoming redundant. A thick plank of understanding had been dragged from under me, leaving me feeling wobbly. I was truly a stranger in these waters.

By the second night out I was relaxing. The sun started to set a little later and dusk was marked every night by a "clunk" that was to become familiar over the next few weeks. This occurred when the rays of the sun weakened and the solar panels finally decided that the day was done and an automatic relay switched them off for the night. That clunk was to be our marker between night and day; for us as potent a punctuation along the path of time as the Greenwich pips. Once heard, it would not be long before thought must be given to the cooking of supper, extra layers of clothing added, barometer checked and sail plan decisions made. I like the day and I like the night, but the bit in between always carries anxiety.

The skies were becoming noticeably different. There were cloud formations with which I was not familiar. Sharp-edged towering stacks were more common and the fluffier clouds, like those of home, were more scarce. Here you could be sailing under an arc of grey monotonous cloud one minute, yet ahead discern a sharp boundary between that and a vivid blue sky which would reflect on the sea, giving you a sense of sailing through a tunnel. This arc of cloud could take many hours to reach before you were released into sunshine and a sparkling ocean. Sometimes there was a little sting in the tail as you made the passage from one weather system to another, acting as a reminder that you were in tricky waters, marked by a blast of breeze that sent you scudding along for five minutes or so before falling back to its former self. I suspected that the boat knew it was coming for she seemed to hesitate just before the change in conditions arrived. It was nothing much, just a little hiccup in her progress, but I

136

noticed it. I was getting to know all her little ways. We were well and truly married now.

On the third day out of Mar del Plata, a snowy white bird — probably a tern but I am not good at these things — circled overhead. I watched it power through the disturbed air in the lee of the mainsail before soaring high, then swooping, almost to land on my head. Round and round it flew, never leaving me, as if wanting to play. I will try to be neither superstitious nor sentimental about this, but in the dark days after Nicholas's death I watched the regular visits of such a white bird as it hovered over the place where he died. We live in some isolation out on the often bleak east coast of England, and visiting birds of all kinds are quite common. But this was dazzlingly white with a radiance I had never seen in a bird before. It flew in tight circles, riding the thermals of a summer afternoon, then swooping towards me so close that often I ducked; then back it went to that tragic spot, soaring and diving, holding my attention with such a force that I have no idea how long I watched its antics. Then it was gone. I would have thought no more of it if it had not reappeared the next day, and the day after that. It shows up less often now, so if I see it more than once a year I am happy. It still has the power to hypnotise me.

But it crosses my mind that it might not be the bird that has ceased to return, but me who fails to see it. I will explain. I had never experienced close, personal grief as intense as that which accompanied Nicholas's death, and to those who dread it I would say that it is nothing to fear. Grief works in strange ways, and not all of them are as depressing as you might imagine. I remember it as a time of great awareness and sensitivity and peace. But time passes and grief dissolves into acceptance, and with it sensitivity diminishes. And so that symbol of my grief, the white bird, might have been there, but I no longer had the eyes to see it. The world seen through grief is a different place, but not necessarily a worse one. It has its peace, and its reassurance. And it gives strength. The sight of that white bird of Patagonia, hovering over me, playing tricks to get my attention as it did that afternoon, took me back to those days, and to a place of closeness. I took the appearance of the white bird as a good sign, a reassurance that I was heading in the right direction.

The following day brought a less inspiring kind of bird life to the boat. Chris spotted a poor bedraggled ball of fluff, shivering, huddled on deck in the lee of the liferaft: a dejected little land bird out of its depth on the ocean. I had no means of identifying it, but it was the size of a robin with a multicoloured chest and black and white tips to its wing. It looked ready to die. There are few sights so pathetic as a lost bird at sea.

Since it was doing no harm we let it stay. It ignored breadcrumbs and there was plenty of rainwater in the scuppers if it wanted any of that. It sat looking at us, probably wondering where the hell it was. It didn't seem afraid. For a while it revived, did a quick circuit of the boat, then flew into the cabin, perched first on the oil lamp then the chart table, visited the kettle, then out again but in a hardly energetic way. We thought that

138

was the end of him and he was playing out the last chapter of his life before falling into the sea exhausted, to be devoured by a ravenous gull.

A couple of hours later he returned, though, bringing his mate with him. There were now two of them, both identical, both bedraggled, both with a look of finality about them. When next we looked there was just one of them, and that hardly able to balance on the swaying deck. The other was nowhere to be seen. Darkness fell and sail trimming and navigation took our attention. The next time we looked, he was gone too.

It is Darwin who is credited with the idea of the survival of the fittest, even if the phrase itself was the inspiration of the philosopher Herbert Spencer. Darwin himself said, "It is not the strongest or the most intelligent who will survive, but those who can best manage change." Darwin approved of Spencer's summing up and later took up the use of it.

Managing the changes that were taking place in his head proved to be Nicholas's final defeat, although God knows he fought valiantly to cope with them. Chris thought the vanishing of the little birds was a Darwinian moment. I thought of my dear boy.

The numbers were not adding up. I measured the distance to Staten Island, where I had decided to break the journey. This bleak chunk of rock 30 miles long lies off the south-eastern tip of the South American continent at the place where the Andes resign themselves and disappear into the depths of the Atlantic Ocean. Allowing for detours while entering and leaving anchorages, and factoring in the help we might get from a current that flows south, and hindrance from bad weather, I was concerned about the little amount of fuel we had left.

I noticed, too, that the water maker had broken. This useful device takes undrinkable seawater and turns it into potable tap water by passing it through filters under much pressure — a procedure described as reverse osmosis, but I have never understood what that meant. I know enough about pressurised systems to understand that if there is a leak then the whole thing fails, and this is what had happened. Off the Patagonia coast did not seem an ideal place to attempt repairs, so we washed up in salt water and gave the plates a quick rinse in fresh. We rationed our personal washing in favour of Baby Wipes. Only the kettle was free from all restrictions.

It was inevitable that in the course of this 1,200-mile passage we would be on the receiving end of several decent gales. We were now in the Roaring Forties at 45 degrees south, although sheltered from the west to some extent by the South American landmass 50 miles away. This cuts both ways, though. By keeping less than 20 miles offshore you can sail in relatively smoother water than if you were further out, since the wind does not travel the distance needed to build steep waves. Even so, you are coming under the growing and often malevolent influence of the speedway track along which the low-pressure systems thunder. They have formed in the Pacific, their tempers worsened after rattling around Cape Horn, and now they spin their way across the Atlantic with the speed of barrels rolling down a steep hill. Winds well in excess of gale force are common here. In fact, a gale on its own would hardly be remarked upon.

We bowled along comfortably in 26 knots of wind from the north-west. Technology has given us all manner of instruments for measuring our performance and progress, but I know of no needle that can register comfort. I measure it by how easy it is to make a cup of tea: does the mug sit easily on the galley, can I pour with one hand holding the kettle and the other the mug with no fear of falling over, can I pour the milk and get most of it in the mug? Can I then get the completed mug of tea to the cockpit with no spillage? If I can do all those things then we are having an easy ride of it.

I had been watching the barometer, which had been making a long, steady fall all day, even though the wind had held true both in strength and direction. What did that mean? I didn't know because somewhere round about the equator someone rewrote the meteorological rule book. At home we would expect a steady increase in wind strength, but I had no clue as to how the portents hereabouts were to be read.

We were now off the Valdes Peninsula, one of the most prolific whale-breeding grounds in the world, and we were there at the right time of year because it is in October and November that they come here to breed. The peninsula itself is barren, though we never saw it, and has been declared a UNESCO World Heritage Site due to visiting orca and the southern right whale, which is endangered. There are elephant seals and sea lions to be found amidst this area of bays, cliffs, mudflats and lagoons. Well, we saw not a single one of them. Possibly they stayed closer to the shore to delight the paying tourists, but no whale showed itself to us.

We rolled on through the blackest night ever, relieved by neither the sight of a star, a light on a distant shore, nor even a far-off ship. Black sky met black sea met black night in a seamless joint. It became colder, and the butter became hard to spread, while the washing-up seawater flowed bitterly cold from the pump, chilly enough to make your finger ends numb. We were sailing into a distinctly different world, of that there was no doubt. Phosphorescence played spookily on the surface of the water as if thousands of stars had dropped out of the sky and were bobbing along the surface of the sea. The sea dazzled in the disturbance left by the passing of the boat as if we were throwing glistening jewels off the stern. This is the handiwork of millions of plankton-like creatures which emit light when agitated, and is no subliminal effect. It is bright and dazzling and distracting and usually associated with warmer waters than these. Some say it is a defence mechanism and the plankton emit this flash of light when under threat. There are, apparently, some full-sized fish that can also pull off this trick, but in their case they emit a glow from their undersides which matches the light in the water around, making them invisible to predators when seen from underneath. Clever, and Darwinian again.

After five days we were ready for a break, having taken three-hour turns to be on watch, which is a tiring regime. For some miles now I had my eye on Isla

Leones on the north-eastern tip of the Golfo San Jorge as a place where we might make a stop-over. It had rave reviews for its safety and shelter and was hardly a detour from our direct route. These are all the necessary ingredients for a happy anchorage.

I altered course. Evening was beginning to turn to night and the fair wind was brisk, and in a moment of overconfidence I made a fatal error in assuming that we would arrive while it was still dark. This rocky shoreline is no place to be feeling your way around in anything less than clear visibility so I rolled in some headsail and slowed the boat down with a good eight hours to go. Wasn't it the perfect invitation for the wind to head us and stall our progress?

With just 30 miles left to go the wind came inevitably from the west, our intended direction. We started to beat, hauling in our sails, edging closer on each tack. In the dawn, the outline of the shore and the islands became clearer. We could have been at anchor and having breakfast by now if I had pressed on instead of slowing down, and that thought nagged as the boat bucked her way towards the shore, cold spray flying. Land revealed itself to be bleak, craggy rock the colour of sandstone with just a little grass here and there, but not a standing tree to be seen. There was no evidence of a human being and no fences or walls to suggest livestock farming. There was nothing, in fact. It was flat, arid and desolate. While Chris slept, I made myself a hasty breakfast and took a steaming mug of tea into the cockpit, then took in a reef to keep her sailing fast but upright. Rocks were in our way and had to be dodged. A passage between the island and the land must be located and the ferocious tide that swept through it had to be allowed for. But despite those pressures, the requirements of coastal navigation were refreshing after the somewhat monotonous routine of ocean sailing, and the blazing morning sun added only to the satisfaction of this landfall.

The island slowly disassociated itself from the mainland. Atop it stood a lonely lighthouse, the most forlorn of that species I had ever seen. I thought it odd that we had not seen its light in the night, and even more curious that the ever-vigilant coastguard had not called us up on the radio with a long list of their pointless questions, as is their habit. I checked our radio set. It was switched on. As we worked our way closer to the shore, through the binoculars I could see rust streaks running the full height of the structure, and broken glass in the windows that surrounded the lantern. Next to it was some housing but the windows were shuttered and no Argentine flag flew from the pole. We had arrived at a place so unfrequented that no one thought it worth marking its presence any longer. The last light had been extinguished. This was to be our first real taste of nowhere.

Then "nowhere" became even more remote as a sense of being on planet Earth slipped from our grasp and we might as well have been on the moon. The coast became dustier, ever more barren and desolate. The tide swept us through the narrow Canal Leones, as the channel between mainland and island is called. No sooner had it spat us out to the west than we turned sharp to starboard heading for an unseen cleft in the rocks, which promised a safe and spectacular anchorage behind. There was no evidence of it, though, as we steered directly for the coordinate marked on the chart. Ahead was a broad bay with a sandy beach; the kind of place where, at home, someone would have been walking their dog, but here it was deserted. A swell broke with an occasional thunder on rocks lurking not far below the surface on our port side. Doubts soon begin to gather. I saw no evidence of any kind of harbour, no gap in the shoreline, no flow of water inland. In the end, though, it resolved itself as closeness gave a new perspective and the landscape turns into something more closely resembling the map. It always seems to come right in the end.

We motored into Caleta Hornos, the "Oven", with mouths agape at the scene that opened up. This was a place where time might not matter at all. We had sailed into a chasm; a cleft in the landscape so excessively jagged and forbidding that it might have been born of the vivid imagination of an artist. This was a place from science fiction. The brown earth of the shore closed around us; birds stopped their foraging amongst the low grass and scrub and stared at us. We turned right, then a bit left, and a beach opened up with sheer cliffs behind it. Ahead of us another gorge a hundred feet deep. We anchored and Chris took lines ashore to hold us in position should the settled weather change for the worse. He came back from his shore expedition and reported, "If the world had ended, we'd never know. Not here."

I rowed across to the shore and landed on a pebble beach, making my way inland along a dried-up river bed which wound its jagged way like gorges do when they have been cut by the actions of thousands of years of water flow. Not even the sound of a bird broke the silence, nor could the rustle of the wind in the short, lifeless grass be heard. By way of confirmation that *horno* means "oven," the baked land looked as though it had been cooked for centuries at gas mark eight. The warmth of the day here did not last long, and as soon at the sun dipped behind the cliffs the oven rapidly cooled and we spent a chilly evening round the stove remembering that whatever the air temperature, it is the seawater that determines the warmth of the boat, and the sea was achingly cold. If you fell in it would take more than your breath away.

I heard a thumping in the night; first as a metallic rattle, then a thud. It went away and I dropped back to sleep. Then it came again — rattle, thud, crash. It was tempting to ignore it, especially as it didn't sound as though it had much force to it, but thoughts of drifting on to rocks were on my mind and so I was out of my bunk and reaching for the torch. I played it over the stern where I saw a disturbance in the sea. I aimed the torch into the crystal clear water. A dazzled baby seal stared back at me with a guilty look on its face. It clearly knew that the self-steering paddle was not a toy, and it should not be playing with it at this time of night. Did its mother know it was out? We stared at each other for some time, but he blinked first and swept off.

146

I never seem to be very lucky with wildlife. When a guide book promises "an abundance of . . ." you can bet that on the day I turn up they will be otherwise engaged. So, with little expectation of seeing penguins, I raised the anchor next morning to cross to where the pilot book promised a colony of them. "There's one!" shouted Chris, as we motored inwards to an anchorage between the outer ends of a bay. An indignant bird stood up and revealed itself to be something else completely — not a penguin at all. We landed and walked carefully ashore, picking our way between collections of animal bones — seals', I imagined. Then, out of the scrub waddled a couple of penguins. Not large, not like the big boys who live in Antarctica, no higher than a foot or so, like model penguins. They weren't in the least surprised to see us, or if they were they didn't show it. They didn't make any kind of fuss, as wild creatures might be expected to do in the company of invading humans. You could convince yourself that they were pleased to see you. How nice to have Sunday visitors, they might be thinking. So where have you come from? From England? Do you have penguins there? Only in zoos. Zoos? What are they? Best you don't know.

All lands of unspoken conversations flashed between me and one penguin in particular who stood his ground as I approached, dipping his head so he could stare intently at my boots. I called him the Bishop because his feathers formed a white band round his neck like a priest's dog collar. We exchanged a few polite words, then, with what seemed like a shrug, he waddled off towards the sea. Not threatened, but possibly bored.

A stroll through the scrub revealed more Magellanic penguins, all the size of a small dog sitting upright on its hind legs. They are creatures with high moral standards and mate with the same partner year after year, even returning to the same nest to lay their eggs. It is enviable family stability. But God does not seem to reward the poor penguin for their decent behaviour. The fish that are their staple diet are moving away from the coasts of Argentina and they must swim further to catch them to places where oil spills might overtake them. Twenty thousand a year die that way off this coast alone.

What is it that makes us feel so close to penguins that we can almost consider them to be one of us? I cursed my ignorance, not only of the penguins and the way they lived their lives, but my lack of real knowledge of the geography, the geology, the sociology, any kind of understanding you care to name of the place in which I was standing. Voyaging should be more than this. It is not intended to be a device for taking us on trips to places where we can stand and gawp and come away none the wiser — that's tourism. Voyaging is a quest not just for distance but to gain understanding, and I silently promised those penguins that I would take the first opportunity to learn more about them and the place where they lived. They nodded their appreciation before turning their backs on me and flip-flopping back to the sea.

I had learned a lesson in that short hour spent on their island, and it was about far more than penguins. For a voyage such as this to be considered a success required more than the mere process of getting the boat from A to B and seeing some sights along the way. It needed to provide a proper education about the places through which I was sailing, or what would be the point?

But the stare of the penguin's eyes had done far more than teach me that lesson. Those brief moments of communication, of me looking in amazement at him and him looking back at me with studied indifference, had crystallised in me a deeper desire for the kind of exploration this voyage might yet offer. It had been sloshing around inside me like an ingredient for a feast yet unmade. I left that island strengthened and more ambitious. Penguin power had done it.

The wind had been forecast to blow from the west, as it usually does hereabouts: swinging from north-west through to south-west and back again as the depressions roll through. The forecast was for no wind of any great strength for the next twenty-four hours, but with the possibility of something stronger after that. We were now faced with the 120-mile crossing of the Golfo San Jorge, a deep indent in the coastline which provided a fetch of over a hundred miles from the west over which steep seas could build. It was no place to be in a gale.

It was late afternoon as we dragged ourselves away from the penguins and set sail southwards to find the

149

wind in the north-east and freshening. We were soon grabbing reefs and much canvas disappeared before the boat felt snug and at ease with the new conditions. It was unsettling; the wind direction was at odds with the forecast and I started to wonder what was going on. On the other hand, it would mean a fast passage across the gulf. On my night watch, when Chris was asleep, with the seas building from astern and the boat galloping southwards with a fine roll, I found myself sitting in the cockpit and declaring to the sky, "I'm enjoying this." I had no fear of being there, nor of what might be to come. Penguin power again?

But doubt always returns, as it should, for it is as good as a life-jacket to a sailor. I had no real experience of heavy weather in this boat and was uncertain how to face it. I did not know how to set the boat and her sails to the sea so that she might have the easiest and safest passage. I could make a good guess, but I still had my doubts. With a gale now forecast we spent a nervous day and there was a growing tension visible on Chris's face. At dusk, having crossed the gulf and once again in the lee of the land, we were close to the shore. We were off Puerto Deseado, earlier known as Port Desire, although those who have been there have reportedly found little to crave. It had crossed my mind that we might refuel there, but the effort taken to do the paperwork, fight the tide in and out, and all the other things that eat away at time when you are in harbour, was time better spent at sea making progress. In the dusk the distant lights did look tempting, though. To provide distraction, a Navy patrol boat asked who we were and what flag we were carrying. I was uncertain how the mention of the British flag, the Red Ensign, might go down with the Navy of a recent enemy, but after a polite interchange they went on their way.

It was eight o'clock that night when things started to deteriorate. I had been warned that weather changes quickly here, and it proved to be the case. After a blast from the north-west, which caused us no trouble, the wind switched in an instant to the south-west and headed us. I watched it climb past 25 knots towards 30, through that barrier and then quickly up to 35. It had taken about a quarter of an hour to reach a full gale. For a little while we sailed on, heavily reefed. It is waves that hinder a boat's progress in strong weather, not the wind alone. It was not long before the seas were building in sympathy to the strengthening wind and any attempt to make progress against it was fast becoming futile.

I hove to. This is a remarkable trick which restores calm to your little ship in a way you would not believe possible if you weren't there to experience it. By removing the headsail, leaving the mainsail up but greatly reduced in size, and pointing the boat towards the wind, she will sit there like a duck bobbing along the water. What had been a violent motion below decks is suddenly stilled and peace is restored. The wheel can be lashed and the boat left to its own devices, rising and falling as the seas pass under her with little upset to those below. The usual practice, if you should find yourself in this position in the middle of the ocean, is to go to bed. What else is there to do? I considered it but

Chris said he was in need of sleep and he would not have rested with both of us with heads on pillows. True, there is the possibility of another ship coming your way, but we had seen only one other vessel for ten days now and it seemed a remote possibility. I took up my watch sitting in the cabin steps with the hatch closed over me and spent most of the three hours with my eyes shut. I don't think that is irresponsible. It is not the kind of sleep that divorces you totally from the world. The slightest change in the sound or motion of the boat would have had me on deck like a shot, whether I was rising from those steps or shooting out of my bunk.

I felt very content with the way the boat behaved. There was no crash of water on the decks, no flinging of her hull by the waves. It was rather peaceful, if tiring, way of sitting out a gale. I quite liked it. Chris seemed less relaxed. When I woke him at seven the next morning, I was standing in the galley giving attention to the cooker.

"Bloody hell," he cried. "I've been lying here working out my chances of survival and you're cooking scrambled eggs!"

CHAPTER
THIRTEEN

THROUGH THE FURIOUS FIFTIES

I can hardly bear to remember the look of deep and utter dismay on Chris's face when I broke the bleak news that another gale was on the way. It spoke of profound gloom. There was little joy to be read in his expression, and not much celebration in my voice as I announced it. The barometer had started its long, steady decline, and that could not be argued with. It was only twenty-four hours since the last gale and we had been making good progress and were now due west of the Cape of the Seven Virgins, moving ever further from land, and sailing into the land of daunting names — Magellan Strait, Le Maire Strait, Staten Island. These are the places that are spoken of in hushed tones; places where you would come for the ultimate staging of *The Tempest*. We were now well and truly amongst them, small part players in the most theatrical stretch of the whole Atlantic Ocean.

I wondered why I was there. Is the point of testing yourself to make yourself stronger? Does the act of testing yourself have a similar effect on your "pluck" as the physical one that makes your leg muscles stronger by running? How would that account for those who face challenges but fail in the face of them? I suppose it's the same as running out of breath; your bravery muscles simply haven't had the exercise they need to keep up the pace. This may be the reason why people who commit brave acts never see themselves as being anything out of the ordinary, for they can only see things from their already brave perspective. They're never out of breath. It was often said to me that this voyage was a "brave thing to do." I genuinely did not understand what they meant, for "brave" is the very last virtue I see in myself.

I congratulated myself on shunning Puerto Deseado and not being drawn into it — Port Desperado, I called it. It would, admittedly, have been convenient to get more diesel and remove at least one pressure, and a drink in a warm bar and a meal that wasn't out of a tin would have been nice too. But there is a rhythm to voyaging, and although the temptation is huge the concentration is best not broken. I heard later that it is something of a dump anyway with little to offer, and together with complex tides and shallows to negotiate, it was as well we decided to press on. Dumps should not be disregarded, however. I can find endless enjoyment in a real hole of a place. I remember feeling cheated when, way back north of Rio, the crew favoured the resort where the beautiful and rich of Rio hang out while I had been more drawn to a nice anchorage near a cement works. To sit in a cafe, even if a dreary one, where men eat fresh from a shift is, for a few moments, to get a little deeper beneath the tanned skin of this place. Not far beneath the skin, perhaps, but it can be more revealing than the thong of a Rio babe.

Change of watch, especially at night, was becoming a miserably cold business. I could not fathom how Chris survived without mugs of hot tea, which I drink with the fervour of an addict. I might get through two every watch, three if it was chilly. I couldn't persuade him that a hot mug of tea is more than a drink, it is a friend offering comfort for both the fingertips and the gullet, and perhaps a reminder of the comforts of home. He preferred to sip at his insipid cold water. I had to give him extra blankets at night. I wasn't surprised he needed them, with no hot tea inside him. Water was becoming in short supply and we were now taking stringent conservation measures. I had a homemade device, shaped like a bag with a hosepipe attached to an outlet at the bottom, which I could hang from the end of the boom to catch rainfall, but there wasn't any. It was cold, cloudy and stormy but it was never wet with rain, although everything else was soaked in salt spray.

Although the barometer was falling ever further, the wind remained very light so the surface of the sea was hardly ruffled and the reflection of the crystal clear stars could be seen in it. As so many times in the true blackness of the nights, there was no line between the sea and the sky, no smudge of demarcation to suggest where one began and the other ended, and so we appeared to float in an encompassing bowl of stars above us that wrapped themselves around us and beneath us. We were floating in something that was no longer mere water.

I was thinking about courage and what it is that makes us strong at times and weak at others. I thought again about the effort of coping in the weeks after Nicholas died. I could have been weakened by it, even destroyed by it. But I had a determination, and I said over and over to myself, "Some good must come of this." Perhaps that outcome is this voyage. So I must make it a good one.

The light weather lasted for thirty-six hours, somewhat to my surprise and the barometer's. The light airs, though, proved as testing as any gale with the sails and the gear slatting around, nagging both themselves and us. The shortage of diesel was on my mind too or I would not have hesitated to motor on. The clouds started to wear an oppressive look; a frown that spelled trouble. Although the barometer had yet to bottom out, indicating a change in wind strength and direction, I guessed that the blow would not come before it started to rise. I was slowly beginning to fathom the way the weather worked down here. I did not disagree when Chris suggested we needed to be anchored somewhere, and soon, for we both needed this rough and cold leg of 1,200 miles from Piriapolis to be over. We sailed on as fast as the sails would take us. The wind stood firm but fair and was bowling us along, mercifully allowing us to sail our selected course.

At dawn, the most sinister landmass I have ever seen appeared out of the mist. It was Staten Island, or Isla de los Estados. To call the facade of this island merely "jagged" is to hardly do it justice. In outline against the flat morning light, it looked as if it had been hastily ripped from a piece of cardboard and dropped in the sea. With its threat, though, came an undeniable majesty. It stood before us like a string of cathedral spires; a landscape too big to appreciate in one gulp. The Andes' final plunge into the ocean certainly brought a drama with it. It was Richard Walter's job to record Anson's disastrous voyage round the Horn in 1740 and he wrote, "...*it is seemingly entirely composed of inaccessible rocks, without the least mixture of earth or mould between them. These rocks terminate in a vast number of ragged points... surrounded on every side with frightful precipices, and often overhung in an astonishing manner. Nothing can be imagined more savage and gloomy than the whole aspect of this coast.*" I have not much to add to that except to say it has malice too. This has been a graveyard to countless ships; the square-riggers without the nimbleness to face the weather that a modern yacht might dance through. Staten Island was rightly feared every bit as much as its close companion, Cape Horn. Mist and low cloud can quickly descend here, and with unpredictable currents it can provide a violent end for the unlucky as they are dashed against its unforgiving coast. So bleak is the place that survival here might be a worse option than death. There have been attempts to make settlements, although none survive apart from a lightly staffed Argentine naval hut. Nature shows no kindness. I tried hard to see anything comforting but its

3,000-foot-high mountains stared blankly back at me, daring me to come any closer, daring me to sail within their grasp. It felt like a slumbering sea monster ready to wake with violence.

I set a course for Puerto Hoppner, a bay of safety on the northwestern tip. It is one of those teasing anchorages of which you can be entirely unaware until you are almost upon it. Sailing on, closing the coast, we passed a barren little island on which surf was breaking. The black cliffs were closing in on every side. Birds stopped their flying to watch us approach. The mountains towered ever higher over us. The silence was painful, overpowering, broken only when the sails were dropped with a rattle and the engine started with a clatter. I felt like apologising for every sound we made, it felt an intrusion. We were in flat water now but our journey was far from done, for we had yet to travel deep into this island's throat. To achieve proper shelter we must allow ourselves to be swallowed by it. I was briefly in favour of anchoring in some shelter off a convenient beach, then gathering our strength for a tricky bit of navigation ahead, but this was largely cowardice and really I knew that what lay ahead had to be faced, and now. Chris asked why we didn't press on and I could come up with no coherent answer.

To pass to the inner lagoon you sail through the narrowest of gaps, hardly wider than your boat. To add interest, and to ensure your pulse is working flat out if it is not already off the scale, there is a rock in the middle of the passage over which the tide flows at breathtaking speed — your engine would not be able to fight it. To add to the growing list of uncertainties, there was also some discrepancy between two pilot books about the depth of water in the gap at the state of tide we were attempting it. One said we would be fine, the other didn't.

At first I could see no gap in the cliffs at all and felt certain we were sailing up a dead end but eventually a cleft, a very small one, did appear. This is where you swallow hard. It looked tight. Talk about putting ships in bottles, this was shaping up to be a similar, delicate insertion. I could see whirlpools formed by the outward rushing of the ebb tide, but within a split second I sensed the adverse current grip the boat and I pushed the throttle. If we were to lose steerage way now we would be swept broadside on to that midstream rock where we would lie, pinned to it with inevitable damage. We had to get through this in one piece.

I took a deep breath and drove us through fast, the exhaust roaring and belching black smoke, and within a few seconds we emerged unscathed on the other side with both of us cheering mightily. "How much depth did it show?" Chris asked. "No idea," I replied. "I had my eyes closed!"

If we had sailed through what felt like the gates of hell, it was to achieve a true heaven. We had barged through the wardrobe door and found Narnia spread out before us. That sense of pure magic that only unspoilt nature can create was all around this place: in the mountains, on the sea, across the sky, around the land. Every sense in my body was telling me this was a special place and like no other I had ever sailed to. Here the howling wind was absent, rebuffed by the high, snow-capped mountains all around. The water across which we sailed was flat and the hell of the open ocean was now elsewhere, on the far side of the wardrobe door. We heard a roar from ahead. It was a deep rumble that spoke of some kind of natural strength. As we rounded the tip of a small island, above us a waterfall cascaded from a great height, emptying with a thunder into a small lake clinging to the mountainside a hundred feet above us. We crept behind a protective island littered with stunted, leaning trees into a spot so snug that no force of nature could disturb us here. We had travelled the wild waves and total peace and shelter had been our reward. I gazed, open-mouthed, at the bare mountain tops, the vivid green of sphagnum swamps, the shimmer of the beech trees.

Chris took lines to rocks on the island to limit our swing, then scrambled up through the steeply wooded shore to take pictures. I sat in the cockpit and enjoyed the intensity of the loneliness. I stared at this perfect vision painted in mountains, water and sky. It is strange how malevolence seen from a distance can melt into comfort on approach. I felt a tingle run down the back of my neck when a thought crossed my mind — this was no longer a mere voyage, it was becoming a living fable. Or was that too fanciful? No, this was now an unfolding story set in mythical landscapes where events were working their way to some kind of grand finale, although what that might be was yet unknown. An unravelling of the Song's End enigma, I dared to hope.

160

Something more practical was also emerging from this new phase of the voyage. It had been mostly an ocean-crossing affair for much of the preceding thousand miles or more, but it was now turning into a coastal adventure. There were rocky obstacles ahead, and diverting tides and currents all to be negotiated. We had been painting on a large canvas but now we must pick up a finer brush and attend to more detailed work.

Our exit from Puerto Hoppner was every bit as tense as our arrival. Even more so because impatience had brought me to the narrow entrance an hour earlier than would be ideal to face the tide. Again, I pushed the throttle as far forward as it would go and in another cloud of black smoke we ploughed our way against a ferocious incoming stream and back into the rise and fall of the ocean swell, which soon toyed with us once again. In a quick backward glance, I thought that I had seen the most magical anchorage of my life so far. I had glimpsed a truly promised land.

With a good forecast for a crossing of the notorious Le Maire Strait, I estimated it would be just a few hours before we were on the mainland side and the anchor could go down once again. No more night watches, no more broken sleep. Yet an uneasy feeling remained, which was crazy, because why should a short 20-odd miles unsettle me when we have just sailed over a thousand? Chris looked moody with his headphones on. He said he was listening to Leonard Cohen, to cheer himself up.

I have often found that when confronting some of the most fearful bits of water, so much care and attention is given to them that they usually pass off with no trouble at all, and you are left wondering what all the fuss was about. So it proved once again. The pilot book warns that an ebb tide here against a gale of wind can, in parts, produce standing waves 10 metres high. These are, effectively, walls of water. A normal wave, even a large one, will appear to advance towards you, at which point your boat will rise to the crest and forge its way through the foam, then you slip down the other side ready to face the next. In standing waves, the apparent movement of water towards you does not happen. It just stands there, daring you to scale it, and so you have to climb these near vertical cliff-faces of sea and slither down the precipitous slope on the other side, like mountain climbing in slippery shoes. A slight error in the steering has you lying "across the slope" where you can quickly tumble beneath the breaking crests of water, never to be seen again. Many ships, and substantial ones, have been lost that way in the Le Maire Strait. But the only waves to confront us were the ripples left by the seabirds as they scattered on our approach. The air was clear too, and we could see both sides of the channel, as far north as Cabo San Diego on the mainland, where the worst of the overfalls are to be found. We motored most of the 16 miles to anchor in Bahía Buen Suceso, in literal translation "good event" or "good success", which it certainly felt like. The Le Maire Strait itself was named by the Dutchman Willem Schouten in 1616. The name of his ship, *Eendracht*, translates as "concord", so together with "good event bay" this seemed to be a place of optimism, despite its bleak and tempestuous geography suggesting otherwise. This also was our landfall on Tierra del Fuego. We were now in the Land of Fire.

Darwin seemed as chuffed to get here as we were, arriving in December 1832.

A group of Fuegians (indigenous Indians living primitive lives) were perched on a wild point overhanging the sea; and as we passed by they sprang up, and waving their tattered cloaks sent forth a loud and sonorous shout . . . just before dark we saw their fire and heard their wild cry.

And so did we, but it was only the call on the VHF radio from the Argentine Navy asking, politely, who we were and what were our intentions.

Buen Suceso is no more than an open bay, but well sheltered from the west and we felt safe. The anchor went down and our greatest friend, the diesel heater, was immediately lit. Its consumption of diminishing fuel was ignored in favour of comfort. At the head of the bay stood a forlorn tin shed, about twice the size of a garage and painted red with white window frames through which we could see glimmers of light. From a white flagstaff flew the Argentine flag and around the establishment — from which could be heard the throb of a diesel generator — was the pointless white fence that the military always love. It was the naval lookout post from which the radio call had come. We passed our details and the young voice asked where we were heading. I said Ushuaia but added that we were concerned about the weather. "We are worried too," he said. "We can only get out of here by boat, and if the weather is bad the boat from Ushuaia will not come." We never met them, but usually this remote station is manned by a handful of young recruits who have to serve their time in this isolated spot accessible only across an uncertain sea. There is nothing for them to do but call up passing ships and yachts and log their passage. That's all. No wonder they were worried that their escape might be delayed.

Our escape was put on hold too. We sailed out the following morning, feeling invincible now and believing the hard bit to be behind us with just a coastal cruise ahead. How foolish. I should have read the small print more carefully, for then I would have noticed that around the very last headland before the Beagle Channel itself the book warns that the tides would be flowing constantly against us at no less than 3 knots. With our speed at somewhere between 4 and 5 in a rising wind, it was going to be slow progress. We edged closer and as we did so the, wind strengthened to a hearty force five and showed signs of more anger to come, betrayed by the gathering dark clouds ahead. With wind and tide directly against us it seemed that this might be one headland too many. Chris stared at the compass and said he was crunching some numbers in his head. It was getting rougher and the first tack gave us a good soaking. We settled on to the offshore tack, losing a lot of ground in the sluicing tide now against us with the speed of a river in spate. Calculations done, Chris declared we were losing ground on every tack and our progress forwards had slipped into the negative. He was probably right. Watching our progress against the land it was clear that every long, wet tack off shore brought us back only to the same spot on the land, and possibly not even that. However, that was not the only reason I decided to turn tail. To turn back for shelter is no disgrace in these places; better men than us have done it. Soon, the anchor was down again and the lads from the Navy welcomed us back with a cheery call on the radio. The diesel heater was lit once again as the wind started to practise its howling, giving it full voice in the night ahead. We felt safe, though.

The next day it was calm. Such is the way of sailing. Why do we never wait till we can make it easy on ourselves? Chris had not slept well; the rattle of the anchor chain as it stretched and groaned in the bow roller in the early part of the night had allowed him only a nervous rest, and he looked wiped out. Having spent a small fortune on a heavyweight anchor (Manson Supreme) and hauled it all the way from England for occasions such as this, and in the foolish belief that money buys you security, I slept soundly and got away with it. As I motored southwards with ease to what the day before had been an unreachable Cabo San Pío, Chris slept.

The early morning sky was brighter to windward and I was abreast that nasty little headland in a fraction of time it had taken to get to the same place the day before. The flow was still against us but it seemed far less urgent and we made good progress. The needle on the diesel tank crept ever lower while the wind failed to deliver anything useful at all.

Gulls hovered in our wake; inquisitive in their swooping and diving, as if they were trying to make some kind of contact. In every one of them, in every bird that keeps us company, I still see Nicholas. I can't help it. I have tried to dismiss this ridiculous romanticism, but I cannot rid myself of the habit. I read it as his welcome to the Beagle Channel.

Distant islands, which were once mere blurs of grey on the far horizon, slowly took shape. The headlands slipped behind us as we lost the adverse grip of the tide and I felt as if I had been given a free-entry ticket to the Beagle Channel. Or perhaps not, for the weather forecast was again looking poor and strong headwinds looked a certainty. A weary and depressed Chris seemed convinced that we would be blown back all the way to Buen Suceso, but I felt more confident. There again, I had not overdosed myself on Leonard Cohen. We had options and I started to examine the chart for places where we might hide and save the precious progress we had made. Chris had been looking at the chart, too, while I read the pilot book. A large open bay, Bahía Aguirre, lay to the north. The eastern side of it appeared rocky, treacherous and unsheltered. The west side, called Puerto Español, looked to be a good haven, though, and has proved to be such over many centuries. But I wanted to press on. We could yet make the shelter of the Beagle Channel before that blow came through.

Hour by hour, the wind edged round till it came from dead ahead and freshened. We were now tacking in growing darkness, a rising wind and ever rockier waters. Darkness fell and we went through the familiar evening routine of feeding ourselves from what was now becoming a dreary food supply — a lot of dull, red sauce met mountain of stodgy pasta.

It was about midnight and I was in my bunk but could not sleep. Chris was on watch. I could hear the wind blowing, but not strongly. Then I heard the repeated rattle of the mainsail and the grinding of winches that showed Chris was reefing. I listened. There was a pause, then he hauled in the mainsail and I felt the boat sail on. Then I heard more cracking of canvas. He appeared to have changed his mind. The winches turned again but this time more slowly. Chris was reefing once again. I came on watch. We were reefed down to the tiniest scrap of canvas, yet the wind was hardly fresh and the boat was barely moving through the water. Chris had the blank look in his eyes of a man who was thoroughly exhausted. He had lost it. I decided to abandon the Beagle Channel and head north and find shelter.

Chris steered while I remained glued to the green glow of the radar screen. There was a feeble light on Cabo San Gonzalo to our left, but after that came a shoal of unmarked rocks and I had to put complete trust in the GPS and charts, the precision of which can be dubious in places hereabouts. The water flattened as we edged into the lee of the rocks, but I never saw them. The sounder started to drop, showing shallower water, and the radar said that there was now land on three sides of us — shelter. The wind dropped to a whisper to prove it. The anchor rattled on to the seabed. It felt as if the right choice had been forced upon us and we both went to bed relieved.

When the next morning dawns calm yet the forecast speaks of 40 knots of wind, what do you do? Chris took to the dinghy, having seen a wooden shack on the shore and wondered if we might beg a few litres of diesel. I gave him the walkie-talkie, just in case, and watched him as he made the long row. While drinking tea in the cockpit, I felt a breeze on the back of my neck and sensed the boat swing till she was pointing in a new and unfamiliar direction. The wind had gone into the east. This was good news, and bad. A fair wind hereabouts is not to be wasted, but equally the winds can play tricks and this gentle breeze could become a gale within half an hour and Chris could find himself stranded ashore. I called him on the radio. He said there was no diesel, only a collection of near derelict wooden houses in pretty poor shape with animal skulls nailed to the walls, either for innocent decoration, or possibly for more sinister reasons. He looked glad to get back on board.

We upped the anchor and sailed for an hour or more but the east wind was only a tease and was soon gone. I felt uneasy. Instincts are best not ignored. I could have pressed on but we turned back yet again, and it was a good job we did for no sooner were we anchored than the west wind was pouring down the mountainsides at speeds of 50 knots, pressing us one way then the other, the anchor chain bar taut but my lovely new anchor not shifting an inch. How I blessed it.

It was time to make tea and read. I learned that the derelict farm buildings that Chris had visited belonged to the estancia, or estate, which had been bought by an 18-year-old Yugoslavian in a fit of romanticism during the gold-rush days of the last twenty years of the nineteenth century. He had collected 44 pounds of the stuff in a nearby roadstead, Sloggett Bay. This exposed stretch of water, about 30 miles to the west of us, was a place where gold could be found "in nuggets as big as kernels of corn," although the gold could only be harvested at a price: the rich seams lay several feet beneath the sand and could only be worked at low tide from ships at anchor. Sloggett Bay provides little shelter and many ships were lost in sudden storms of the kind we were now sitting out. With his new-found wealth he sent for his girlfriend, who came to join him. Contact with the rest of the world was by a navy ship which called three times a year, if they were lucky. Sometimes it never made it. Otherwise it was six days of horse-riding to Ushuaia. A couple needs a good supply of romance to survive in a place like this.

With every gust that shrieked through the rigging, I peered anxiously through the cabin window, up and down like a nervous yo-yo all day. Was this the gust that would finally dislodge the anchor and have us drifting down on to the least hospitable rocks I have ever seen, now just a short mile to leeward? I had picked out two marks on the shore — an unusual-shaped tree I could quickly identify, and a distinctive outcrop of rock half a mile behind it. As long as they stayed in line we were secure. Williwaws, or mini-tornadoes, were spinning

169

across the distant water to the north of us, raising columns of water and leaving streaks of foam on the surface of the sea. They seemed very close.

After our failed departure that morning, I had returned to a slightly different anchorage to the night before, thinking it might provide more shelter, being closer to land and in less open water. This was a mistake. The hills act like accelerators and increase the strength of the gusts; the trade-off is that the water is flatter. I could see a row of abandoned wooden shacks, the wood bleached, and yet more sinister animal skulls nailed to the walls, surviving when all else was crumbling about them. We saw caves too. More reading revealed a depressing truth about this place.

This was where the missionary and navigator Captain Allen Gardiner came to grief. In 1884, traumatised by the loss of his wife, he came to Patagonia to establish a floating mission which would travel the bays and islands, spreading the Good Word amongst the resident Patagonians, who were a wild and uneducated race. Fleeing for their lives from natives intent on killing them, Gardiner and his men were overtaken by bad weather and blown to the precise spot where we were now anchored, off Puerto Español. They took shelter in caves, the ones that were now clearly visible from our deck. In need of food, Gardiner sailed back to Caleta Banner, the harbour from which he had been evicted by the natives, in the sparse remnants of their wrecked boat. It was a piece of considerable seamanship. This exceptionally safe harbour, off Isla Picton, was named by Gardiner from Psalm 60:

"*Though hast given a banner for those that fear thee, that it might be displayed because of the truth.*" A cache of food in barrels had been buried there and he quickly secured it as the natives gathered once again, clutching their spears and intent on murder. Optimistically, Gardiner left a note for any friendly passer-by — "You will find us in Spanish Harbour." He set off back to Español. But no rescue came, the food soon ran out, scurvy and starvation followed. Only their bodies and diaries were found. Gardiner, it was thought, was the last to die. He died in a cave. We could see it.

GRIBs may sound like a particularly nasty infection; in fact, they are the modern navigator's best friend, especially in remote parts not covered by conventional weather forecasts. They are small binary files and can be downloaded to a computer via a satellite phone or some other radio connection. Once decoded and overlaid on a map (easily done), they indicate the wind strength and direction every six hours for up to the next six days. How much you trust them is up to you, for they are the creation of a computer and not a human, but out to 48 hours they are pretty good, provided you understand their limitations.

Having been at anchor for 24 hours we were more than ready to move on, although a glance to seaward was enough to give you a chill, for it remained an unbroken vista of white, tumbling water as a strong gale of wind blew across the fast-flowing tide that had defeated us the day before. It remained like that for the whole day. The diesel heater that evening had been running on its lowest setting to conserve fuel and the constant nagging of the wind had left us tired. It was never quiet, and every lurch of the boat caused us to clench, wondering if this was the one. Chains can break, anchors drag and shackles part. These things are never far from your mind at times like these. We took an early night, but not till I had downloaded the latest GRIB file and seen that the following morning, which was a Sunday, the wind would still be from the west but much lighter. I took this on trust, went to my bunk and quickly dived deep beneath my thick duvet, trying to drown out the howling all around. We had agreed on a early start, about first light, anchor up by seven o'clock, and then if things were going well we could make it to the next harbour by darkness. With some urgency, Chris had been thumbing through the pictures in the pilot book and noticed that at Harberton, the next and only possible stop before Ushuaia, several of the pictures featured trucks. Where there are trucks, there is diesel, Sherlock concluded.

I set my alarm for six thirty but by six Chris was already up and about, dressed, and nervously pacing the cabin. I don't think he'd slept at all. "Shall we get this over with?" he said, glumly. I stuck my head out. The wind was well down. It was exactly as the GRIBs had forecast. This meant the sea would be down as well and we might be in for a smooth ride, although I did not dare to hope.

With only 80 miles to go I cannot imagine why we felt daunted at the prospect, but I too shared a little of Chris's obvious apprehension. I think we had expected that when we finally closed the shore after that 1,200-mile passage south, it would be somehow all over. In fact, the struggle was just beginning. As the anchor came up, I glanced at the barometer and saw it was high and steady. The barometer is king around here and I paid due homage.

We motored along in confidence. Breakfast was porridge with a lavish squirt of Golden Syrup, which I always find has a rocket-fuel effect in the morning. I told Chris to get his head back down. He quickly accepted and was soon hard asleep. I motored westwards, diving below now and again to read the level in the fuel tank, and looking all the time for the slightest hint that there might be a little wind and we would be able to sail, for there was certainly not enough juice to get us all the way to Harberton, a good twenty hours away.

A breeze obliged, but only for a while, then the engine went on, then the breeze came back. I could now rise above the irritation of it all, for I was increasingly enveloped in sheer wonderment at the place to which me and my boat were heading. It was like the lifting of a veil. No picture like the one now laid out before me had I seen before.

Its beauty was beyond mere geography. The Beagle Channel is a watery highway between the mountains and the islands stretching to what seemed like infinity. But it took me even further than that; it transported me towards another place beyond. I simply loved it, and it was love at first sight. I sat alone in the cockpit, my trusty companion the tea mug in my hand, and simply thanked God for a place like this.

A long, low swell, like a gently undulating landscape, was creeping up from the direction of the Horn. It disappeared as we edged into the shelter of the islands, each of which gave new delights with fresh scenery of craggy landscapes with snow-laden tops descending through forested hillsides down to the cold, blue water. The air was frigid, but it was the sight of the Beagle Channel that took my breath away.

Relief played a part too. We had made it. We were safe. With luck a bit of wind would get us to the anchorage, still 30 miles ahead. Chris kept his head down till mid-morning and I didn't disturb him. On waking, his face lit with joy for the first time for a long time when I told him how far we had progressed.

The day wore on and we edged further into the narrower and narrower Beagle Channel to be rewarded with what felt like a welcoming hug. By midnight it was time to find an anchorage and the chart work became enthusiastic once again as I navigated us into a safe harbour. We edged towards the shore, guided by a single light on a headland until the revolving green trace on the radar screen showed us to be surrounded by land on three sides.

On the shore, now just 50 yards away, we saw lights from low houses dotted by the water's edge, their glimmer reflected on the rippled sea which became calmer by the minute. The anchor chain rattled away till it found the sea bed, a quick burst of astern from the engine to bury the anchor firmly in the mud in the interests of an untroubled night, and then that moment of almost aching peace when the engine is stilled.

Then, in an instant, the shore lights went out and the village disappeared. It was as if it had never been there. Only the stars shone out.

CHAPTER
FOURTEEN

THE SOUTHERNMOST TOWN IN THE WORLD

The village of Harberton, as you may know, is in Devon, not far from Totnes. Although there is little to compare that English village with Harberton, Argentina, where we were now at anchor, they carry similar blood in their veins. There's a lot of stuff hereabouts from dear old England. We discovered this on landing when we were met with enthusiastic guides. They took us to the first and original wooden house to be erected here, which was originally built in kit form back in Devon and shipped out here (possibly as the world's first ever flatpack house) in the nineteenth century. It was full of surviving furniture that had a certain period English look to it. We were shown the garden, which had the only daffodils to be found in South America, brought from England. Later I spotted in the back of a shed, smothered in dust and droppings and bound in cobwebs, a Triumph Herald, the smart UK car of the 1970s. An explanation of this place was needed. And why did the lights go out? The answer — the generator shuts down at 11.30 sharp.

176

This was the first, and most famous, estancia to be founded on Tierra del Fuego. If this part of the world seems remote now, imagine how it must have felt when Thomas Bridges and his wife, Mary, settled here in 1886. Mary had come from Harberton, Devon, hence the name they gave to this spot. Their son, E. Lucas Bridges, was later to write an account of his childhood in this wild, watery and dangerous land where transport was by water or on horseback across the mountains, and where his parents struggled to befriend and educate the native Indians. It reads like a story where *Swallows and Amazons* meets an evangelical Lone Ranger. His eventual book, considered a masterpiece of its kind, is called *Uttermost Part of the Earth*. Never was there a truer title.

The Bridges were zealous missionaries and for thirty years worked amongst the local population, who were members of one of four tribes: the Haush, Ona, Yahgan or Alacaluf. All shared the same primitive life but the tribes were distinct, each with its own language recorded in dictionaries by Bridges to provide a valuable academic resource. Captain Cook described their conversation as sounding like a man clearing his throat. They were essentially hunter-gatherers seeking guanaco which, to an untrained eye, might appear to be deer or llama. Darwin seemed fond of the creatures: " . . . *if a person lies on the ground, and plays strange antics, such as throwing up his feet in the air, they will almost always approach by degrees to reconnoitre him. It was an artifice that was repeatedly practised by our sportsmen with success.*"

The guanaco fleece is soft and warm and these days considered a luxury fabric, but to the Indians of Tierra del Fuego it was the only cloth they had, and together with guanaco skin was their only protection against a malicious climate. "*Their skin is of a dirty coppery red colour,*" said Darwin, but the Commander of the *Beagle* on her first expedition to these waters was more exact in his description: "*. . . their bodies were smeared over with a mixture of earth, charcoal, or red-ochre and seal oil; which, combined with the filth of their persons, produced a most offensive smell.*" When they tired of eating guanaco, they would search for mussels on the shores of the Beagle Channel. Some used canoes with which to hunt, others not; some painted their faces, some wore no clothes at all. The Yahgans wove intricate baskets and used spears and harpoons to hunt otter, fish and seals, but carried clubs only to use against each other. The Yahgans fished from bark-covered canoes, always paddled by the women, who were the only ones who could swim. The children were placed in the middle of the craft while man, the hunter, took his place in the bow ready to strike. They worshipped no gods, and Bridges sought to remedy that by bringing his God to them, with little apparent success. Their lives were lived in encampments — the Alacaluf, though, were nomadic — and for the early visitors to Tierra del Fuego the only sure sign of the presence of natives was the smoke that rose from their camp fires, or flames seen in the night, hence "the Land of Fire" — Tierra del Fuego.

This is no place for a full retelling of Bridges' story, and it would be wrong to suggest he was misguided in his missionary work. He and his family were truly courageous people. But it is an irony that, having sent word back to England of people living in such apparent squalor and indignity, the British should respond with parcels of clothing on a generous scale. These were distributed and provided unaccustomed warmth to the Indians used to no more than loin cloths. The apparent comfort, though, was no friend. It allowed colds and influenza to incubate, developing into pneumonia against which they had no immunities and it caused many deaths. Diseases too, such as measles, were easily caught from visiting sailors and many died, enough to bring about the eventual demise of these native people. It was we who killed them off. Trying to do good is a complex business.

With the admirable commitment of a Yahgan hunter, driven by his survival instinct and growing desire for this testing passage to be over, Chris set off on a quest for diesel. He clasped my yellow jerry cans as tightly as if they were the key that would release him from his captivity. He was right. Only with more diesel were we ever going to get to Ushuaia. He was lucky. He needed go no further than the jetty before he was met by a surviving member, no less, of the Bridges family, who was standing alongside a somewhat confused old man who eventually got the message. He took our jerry cans and promised to be back within the hour. He sped off in an old truck, clouds of dust in his wake. I couldn't

179

imagine where he was going. This was the least likely place in the world to find a filling station.

Even better news was to swiftly follow, for the word "breakfast" was mentioned with such additional uplifting words as "coffee" and "bacon," and we were pointed in the direction of a hostel/restaurant, newly built and clearly designed by an architect for whom "sympathy with the landscape" was an alien concept. But to hell with such dreary urban stylish preoccupations when there was bacon and eggs to be had, accompanied, rather strangely, by jam tarts, as is the local custom — but we were not complaining. We booked a steak and chips dinner for that night and Chris's eye fell on the well-stocked wine rack, overflowing with rich, smooth and lusty South American reds which he thought would relieve him of the inferior plonk I shipped aboard. I have never sailed with a wine buff before and it makes for testy mealtimes. Small boats are no places for fine palates. Wine boxes will do just fine. All that is required is getting something down your neck that will anaesthetise the hardships of the day just passed. But the wine buff jeers, and wastes his time because it takes so long for him to verbally rid his system of the disgust his palate is signalling that the rest of us are well on the way to oblivion while he is still belly-aching about Great Clarets he once Drank. So I told him repeatedly that I thought the wine boxes were great, fabulous, even though I knew they were pretty disgusting. Terrible behaviour, but as a skipper you must allow yourself a little private sport now and again.

180

The diesel arrived on the back of a rusty red truck that looked as though it had made a long and dusty journey into an outback. I asked where the diesel came from but there was pointedly no reply so I didn't ask again. Nor was there any money to pay for it. We had small Argentine change left over from Mar del Plata, but not sufficient. Now taking on the role of world banker, Chris skilfully negotiated a settlement that involved the poor guy accepting a fistful of dollars, a few British pounds, some pesos and possibly some euros, and any other bit of Monopoly money we could dredge up from the depths of our pockets. There might even have been a bit of Moroccan in there. In fact, I think the old boy got a good deal in the end. He seemed happy enough about it. Chris smiled broadly as the diesel trickled from the jerry cans into the boat's tank. This was his ticket home and why, when we drew alongside the jetty in Ushuaia the following day, I thought he was going to kiss the ground.

Chris was a good crew. He could steer, stand his watches, reef as required, and navigate. Taking on crew is sometimes pot luck and to get even two of those four skills in a crew is rare. But to be a proper sea-going companion takes a little more than the possession of technical skills. I had never sailed with anyone before who did not seem to find any romance in being at sea. I cannot imagine why anyone who was not in possession of a love of it would have anything to do with being on the water. They must find it a miserable business.

181

Chris flew out the following morning on the first flight he could get while I cleaned the boat alone. He wanted sight of Buenos Aires, dismissing Ushuaia as "nothing much more than a tacky ski resort". I saw it differently. This was the southernmost town in the word, and deserving of some respect if only for that reason. This was somewhere I had read about, planned for and had sailed 8,000 miles to achieve, and I was not going to brush it aside so easily. I did what I always do in a new place: try to create a feeling of what it is like to live there and turn myself into an imaginary resident. I build myself a new life in my mind. I shun restaurants and prefer to go shopping. I look for street markets and get a thrill from a supermarket; even a run-down corner shop can hold my interest. The very best, though, is always a hardware shop, and I love to turn over tools and fittings from other cultures. I wander the back streets at dusk and peer into the windows and try and guess how people are leading their lives, what they are eating, how rich or poor they might be, how happy or sad they seem.

These back-street walks can lead to unexpected places. When Nicholas died I was at sea, delivering our boat back to the UK after I had sailed in the 2005 OSTAR. Libby broke the news to me on the satellite phone. I was sitting on the foredeck at the time. The cabin stereo was playing sea shanties. Mercifully, we were only a few hours' sail from Halifax, Nova Scotia, from where I was home in less than 24 hours. The following year I returned to finish the job of bringing the boat back to England and sailed onwards to St

Johns, Newfoundland. I remember walking the suburban back streets there, as I was doing here in Ushuaia, but with a growing conviction that, somehow, this was where he was to be found. I could see exactly where he was. He was in a normal domestic set-up, eating his supper, being nice to his family, living a happy life. Right there! Not somewhere else, but close to me. I did not expect to see him; I knew that was impossible. Nor would I have gone in search of him, for that made no sense either. But I knew he was there, and happy in one of those houses in those back streets, part of a new family, having a new life. I knew it. That conviction has never left me.

In Ushuaia I saw weathered faces, tense from the ravages of cold winds and pale from the lack of sustained sun in a place where, famously, it is said that it can snow on any day of the year. On the plus side, the cold and snow brought a little tourist prosperity; the shops were adequate but not luxuriously stocked, the supermarkets had variety but only just enough. It was a place that was getting by, clinging on for dear life to the edge of the world. People did not linger on the cold streets; even with summer approaching the air every night was full of the sweet smoke of pine-fuelled fires and they were much needed. The next day it snowed and I trudged the mile to the filling station with my diesel cans aboard a borrowed trolley, wrapping myself in several sweaters to keep out the cold. A blizzard blew in my face as I trudged the mile back to the boat, hauling my load like a chilly carthorse that wanted to get back into the warmth of its stable.

I stayed a couple of days, wandering mostly, and doing little jobs to bring the boat back into good order. I took time to befriend local sailors and get advice on this and that and where to go. They were overwhelming with their offers of help, nothing was too much trouble, everything they knew they shared. My boat was something of a sprat compared to the huge, stout charter boats that were now my neighbours. But size counted for nothing here and to speak to their skippers was to be on the same playing field. They knew that to get here from Europe took a bit of effort, and I appreciated the respect they showed.

Ushuaia is not a place to leave a boat to its own devices, though. I was nearing the end of another leg and Christmas was again rolling into sight. Ushuaia, as a harbour, is completely exposed to easterly winds, which are nasty when they arrive, and it does not take long to do damage when a boat is hard pressed against the exposed jetty with a big sea running. The upside is that complete shelter is not far away, but in a different country.

Twenty miles to the east is the small Chilean naval port of Puerto Williams and it was where I had long planned on leaving her. But a couple of problems presented themselves. There is no way a berth can be booked in advance, so if I were to turn up and there was no room, where would I go? Cape Town, or on to Australia? Even if I was able to leave the boat, how would I get back to Ushuaia, from where I had booked a flight? It's fair to say that the Chileans and the Argentinians aren't exactly hostile to one other, but they clearly aren't much in love. There is no regular ferry service across the narrow Beagle and the tourist boat only runs in high summer. They might as well be a thousand miles apart. If I were to sail across, it was possible I might get stuck in Puerto Williams. I wouldn't be the first.

It snowed heavily as I headed east with a fresh-to-strong breeze behind me, filling the headsail, which was the only sail I needed. The wind funnelled between the mountains and accelerated as it blew us into the shelter of Puerto Williams via the many radio operators who quizzed me at every turn on where I had come from, where I was going and how many people were on board. It is never-ending and unnecessary. But the reward was huge. In what seemed like an instant, I was out of the maelstrom of snow, wind and radio chatter and alongside a clutch of other boats, all of them snuggled up to a sunken old ship called the *Micalvi*. The guy in charge, Miguel, a former Chilean lighthouse keeper, who had taught himself English so that he could talk on the radio to passing ships, welcomed us. I asked if I might leave the boat for a couple of months. To my ultimate relief, he declared it to be no problem.

You are never far from paperwork when you cruise in South America and certainly the Argentine Prefectura back in Ushuaia had taken it to new heights. Although they remained at all times courteous, I spent many hours wishing to God that they'd move on from carbon paper. In Chile, in Puerto Williams, things had a different, military feel. This small harbour is the base from which the Chilean Navy, the Armada, patrol their half of the Beagle Channel and adjoining islands. They watch the Argentinians like hawks, and in turn are watched back. It's not exactly a cold war, but it's pretty chilly. Again, the forms were lengthy, obscure and often pointless; but there was much here that was to do with safety and it is no bad thing that they know precisely what equipment you carry on board, and how many days' supply of food and water you have. Translation proved a problem. Simple words like engine, sails, diesel, oil, anchor, I could manage, but others defeated me. A jolly naval officer, rotund and with a giggle, decided the only way he could make me understand was to act out the words; hence whooshing noises into the sky for "flares," feverish rowing for "dinghy". Signalling mirror defeated him. It took an hour to check into Chile. I was told this was almost a speed record.

It was November and spring by now should have been well advanced but there was little evidence. Trees that should be in leaf were still in their deathly winter state, the grass showed no signs of growth, and the horses that roamed free on the gravel streets, shuffling in and out of the gardens with no respect, grazed on what little they could find. Out in the Beagle Channel, the cold wind whipped up white water and the drizzle in the air turned to fine snow. The many dogs were friendly, and those people who were not huddled against the cold nodded in recognition when they met you on the streets. There were several shops advertising themselves as supermarkets and all were similar: they were gloomy, lit only by stark and insufficient florescent tubes. The variety of tinned goods was fine, the fresh fruit less so, and there was no meat or fish to be found that wasn't frozen. The bread came in hard, white bread cakes, for which I developed a fondness and which we were later to name "frisbees". The town is supplied by regular ferry from Punta Arenas, another frontier town on the Magellan Strait, which is three days away. The ferry arrives Thursdays. If you want tomatoes or cabbage, Thursday afternoon when the ferry has unloaded might be your only chance.

I bought bread and eggs — no egg boxes to be found so they rattled in the bottom of the carrier bag — and made my way back to the boat, now snug alongside the *Micalvi*. This is a legendary place amongst sailors who venture to these parts. She is an elderly ship, so tired of life that she rests on the bottom of a muddy creek, no longer bothering to float with the rising tide. But she is not without life for she has been made into the southernmost yacht club in the world and is rightly celebrated. It was a stroke of genius on the part of the Chilean Navy who saw, back in 1961, that it would be a great convenience for visiting yachts to have somewhere to secure alongside in the complete shelter that this creek provides. Dear old *Micalvi* was born in 1925 and served her time in the Baltic, carrying munitions from Europe to Chile, and was ordered to be broken up on arrival, but she survived. She brought miners to support the Chilean Navy mutiny of 1931, worked as a lighthouse tender, got old and rusty, but achieved immortality in Puerto Williams where what remains of

187

her rattles every night to the boisterous conversations of high latitudes sailors.

There were not many of those around this early in the season and I often sat alone in the empty bar, clutching red wine, edging ever closer to a massive log stove that emitted heat like a power station, as I watched a few flakes of snow drift past the brass scuttles. I looked at the numerous flags and banners pinned to walls and ceilings, and recognised the boat names scrawled on some. Those of a Christian belief will say that we shall all meet on the day of judgement, but in the meantime sailors have to make do with *Micalvi*, which, in my estimation, is pretty close to heaven. Sit here long enough and every hardy sailor in the world will come your way.

Less so at the cafe up the hill in what is ambitiously called the "Commercial Centre". This is a row of huts clustering round an unmade square. It is the nearest this place gets to downtown. There is a modest souvenir shop, a coffee shop which had no milk but good cakes, and an ironmonger who did not have a machete, which I was seeking in order to make a knife to cut the heavy green kelp that sticks to the anchor when you raise it. On the plus side, there was a small shop where could be bought sliced bread, if you wanted it, and bits of frozen chicken. The cafe, though, was disappointing. The pictures sticking to the window promised chicken and chips, even fish and chips. I went inside and a lavish and lengthy menu was thrust in front of me. "It is so exciting," the young waitress said, "to have someone to speak to in English." She giggled. "I am trying to

188

learn." She had already mastered a key phrase: "This is the menu, but there is only pizza, and only one kind of pizza. Sorry." Like everyone else, the chef was no doubt waiting for Thursday when his ship comes in.

"You must look out for Denis," I had been advised by a skipper back in Ushuaia. "He will look after your boat." This had promise. To leave a boat in such a tempestuous part of the world as this, 8,000 miles from home, is something of an act of faith, and to know there is one human being on the doorstep who cares is a great comfort. Denis duly appeared on the *Micalvi*, and I liked him straight away. Yes, he would check the lines, open up the boat on dry days to let the fresh air blow through, be around if she had to be moved. He could get gas, do laundry . . . and on it went. A complete one-man service centre.

Procedures had to be gone through, though, and authority had to be assigned to him during my absence. This involved the signing of a lengthy document, not unlike Magna Carta, then processing to the town hall where a government official would give it her official stamp and take a tenner from me for having done so. Denis apologised, embarrassed. I walked up to his house, a wooden bungalow like all the houses here, on the far side of town. It was the only one with a garden; most were surrounded by patches of uncut grass, rubble and general domestic detritus. Denis's house, on the other hand, had flower beds and vegetable patches in neat and tidy arrangements. He was Swiss, which might explain. He was also the most southerly strawberry grower in the world.

Once inside his bungalow, heated by wood, he offered tea from a vast collection of leaves, the collecting of which seemed to be his hobby. His rooms were lined with books, for this was a cultured man making a small living by caring for visiting boats while studying the wildlife and sharing his understanding with walkers and sailors. I saw him again the following day. He was climbing over the guardrails of the *Micalvi*, heading for a small, white yacht I had seen in Ushuaia and which Denis clearly knew. He was clutching a handful of freshly cut chives and was greeted as a long-lost friend. The boat was home to a young French couple. To say they were sailing on a budget was to overstate matters, for I don't think they had any money at all. Most remarkably, she had given birth over the winter, only six weeks back, to a baby which could now be heard gurgling away below decks. As the time for the birth approached, they told me, they simply upped the anchor in some remote Chilean fjord where they had been living for some time, motored to Ushuaia, and popped into the local hospital. Once safely delivered, they and the baby set sail again, for *Micalvi*. They made their own charcuterie, being French, and chunky, garlicky sausages were strewn across the cockpit, dangling on strings from the boom and curing in the clean, dry air. For heating, which was most necessary, they had made their own wood stove, the chimney of which was spewing tar across their decks but they didn't seem to mind. Heroic adventurers come in many shapes and sizes. They looked very happy, and Denis's chives only added to their joy.

I walked in the snow, falling so thick that it was difficult to see more than 50 yards in front of me, and found it exhilarating. This was the final confirmation that I had come to the end of the world. The decks were icy to the point of danger when I got back. The French couple said it was so dangerous that they didn't dare cross the rafts of boats with the baby so took to their dinghy and rowed ashore. The cabin temperature was down to 5 degrees and I struggled to light the sometimes tricky diesel stove. Soon the heat rose to 14 degrees, which at home would be considered chilly, but here, despite the snow falling and the wind howling, it felt like the inside of a baker's oven.

A nagging problem remained. I had to be certain of getting back to Ushuaia to catch my flight and that was not yet guaranteed. I had been introduced to a guy named Atilio in Ushuaia. He was the owner of an elderly but stylish steel ketch and became known in my mind as "the man with the white ketch". He said he would be over on Sunday and was happy to give me a ride back. He was coming to collect kayaks, newly arrived from Punta Arenas on the Thursday ferry. But Sunday brought bad weather and my promised rendezvous moved to Monday. It was getting unnervingly close to my flight time. Atilio reassured me he would be there. Still unconvinced, I checked alternatives. I could fly out of Puerto Williams to Punta Arenas, not to Ushuaia. From Punta Arenas it would be a flight to Santiago and that would mean tearing up the expensive ticket I had already bought, as well as inflicting on me a lengthy tour of the capital cities of

South America. Atilio and his ketch rapidly became my only hope.

Monday wore on. Countless times I stepped ashore and climbed to the brow of the hill to look out across the water to see if the white ketch was coming. Only white horses were in view, no white hulls. Then, at teatime, when I had given up hope, a brave little ship appeared round the headland, storming downwind, seen at first only as a white smudge. But was it the white ketch? In was many minutes before I could resolve the second mast with my eyes. Surely there could not be two white ketches at sea on the same day?

I boarded her the next morning together with a couple of other passengers and found a lovely old yacht with much mahogany below making cabins with wide berths, and a large cabin table above which swung an oil lamp round which we gathered to drink beer and eat nuts before departing. We motored down a flat and windless Beagle Channel, chilly after the sun set turning to very cold by darkness. The cockpit of the boat was small and reduced in size even further because of a large espresso machine that was laid across it. A woman had decided to move her coffee shop from Puerto Williams to the other side of the Beagle Channel. I couldn't work out why. There were no more potential customers on the other side than she had already. In fact, there was nobody at all. I told her I was grateful for Atilio's offer of a lift back to Ushuaia. She replied, "This is the sort of place where we all help each other if we can. That is how it is." And so it was, and so they did, and I was grateful. I pressed money on Atilio, and would happily have given him all the money I had. It was firmly refused.

CHAPTER
FIFTEEN

THE BEAGLE CHANNEL

Another Christmas, another January, another leg begins.

I spent yet another unsettling four-week interlude in the northern latitude winter, the halls bedecked with boughs of holly. It was the approaching southern latitude summer that was more on my mind. I was suffering from acute seasonal displacement. "You're not really here, are you?" my perceptive wife remarked. True, my heart remained in the chilly waters of the Beagle, and there it stayed until a high-speed launch whisked me across the water from Ushuaia and dumped me on the shore for the two-hour truck ride to Puerto Williams.

I was back for the final leg, the long one that promised the wonders of the Beagle Channel, the thrill of the Horn, and the 9,000-mile passage back home. The producers of my television series broke it to me gently that it would not be returning to the screens for at least another seven months. They did so with deep apology in their voices and pain on their faces. Little did they know that I could have kissed them there and then. Of course, I looked downcast. We know, or at least they think, that there is nothing more important than being on the air. Some of us know that being on the water eclipses that thrill a thousand-fold. So I replied with a gloomy but understanding face, told them how sad I was to hear that news and that I would somehow contain my frustration at not having to stand in front of their camera. The instant I turned my back on them my sombre look melted into joy at the thought that I might now be able to fulfil one of my life's greatest wishes. I had long wanted to sail a long ocean passage alone. For the demanding coastal sailing around the Beagle Channel, I would need crew. But once their job was done, the Atlantic Ocean would be mine alone. I was now presented, on a plate, with an opportunity for what could only turn out to be the greatest adventure of my life.

But lots to do to make the dream come true. Six short weeks had made a huge difference to the feel of Puerto Williams and I felt as if I was returning to a different place. Trees were now green, grass flourished, meltwater ran down the hillsides forming crystal clear tumbles of water from which cattle drank. The snow line had risen and something of the winter mystery had melted with it. Navarino Island, which forms a large part of the south side of the Beagle Channel, does not make many concessions to tourism; few venture there except a handful of young backpackers and committed, hardy walkers. The truck that was taking me back to the *Micalvi* rattled along dusty, twisting tracks which ran alongside the Beagle for much of the way. My eyes hardly left it; it had lost none of its magnetic attraction.

I loved it now as much as I did when it emerged from the mist that nervous morning we turned around the toe of South America. Small wooden houses popped up along the roadside and people ran to wave as we passed. What do they do here? How do they earn a living? The inevitable satellite dishes apart, these were scenes unchanged since the pioneer settlements a century and a half ago.

Denis, the sailor's Mr Fixit, had done me proud with his caretaking, and *Wild Song* was exactly as I left her. There was time to reconnect with this dear little town at the end of the world. I had a feeling of coming home. I felt I really lived here. I found my way around as if I had never been away. I discovered two new shops I hadn't seen before, and these followed the pattern of the others in that one had eggs but no milk, the next had milk but no butter . . . and on it goes. Some shops stocked better food than I remembered back in November; cabbages of giant proportions were now abundant. There was no rush this time to light the cabin heater with the days noticeably longer, although the air was sometimes chilly, then mild the next minute, then wet, then foggy. Never the same for long, always changing, a new prospect by the hour. *Micalvi* was as alive as a cattle market with the charter season now in full swing; the bar was packed at nights and to get a chair near the woodstove was a gamble. Denis appeared, this time clutching lush handfuls of parsley and basil — a sure sign of a changing season.

A steel craft of haphazard but robust design lay between me and the *Micalvi*, and her skipper, Chris, knew the Chilean channels inside out. He had skippered the famous *Pelagic*, a rough, tough yacht built for Antarctic waters and owned by Skip Novak, who was taking charter parties round here before anyone else had thought of the idea. He is held in no small respect as a high latitudes sailor. Chris now had this small boat of his own, bought cheaply from a Frenchman, and once the painting was done he was heading off to the Darwin mountains to combine sailing and climbing. He was a Falklander, which presented him with no small difficulty when he tried to enter Argentina. He carries a UK/EU passport, as you would expect. But should the immigration officer in Ushuaia stamp it when he enters Argentina? As it is a foreign passport, the rules say he should, but the Argentines believe the Falklands are theirs and have no need to stamp one of their own citizens on entry. "It ends up with many long phone calls to Buenos Aires," he says with a heavy sigh. "I've given up. I just don't go to Argentina any more." By coincidence, I passed through Buenos Aires on the anniversary of the Falklands invasion on my way back here. I asked the English-speaking hotel receptionist if it would be a good idea to keep my head down. He laughed. "A few people care a lot, but most care very little."

I had not given much thought to the scale of my achievement so far, which some might consider considerable. I was now 9,000 miles from home, yet the relentless pressure of organising crew, spares, flights, hotels and ferries had become all-consuming, leaving no space for wider or deeper thoughts than those relating to getting the boat from A to B, and eventually home. But that may not be a bad thing, for there's not much to be gained from reflecting on how well you've done so far. One of the rules of voyaging is to look forwards and never backwards. Simply to be here, even if I got no further, would not be a bad effort, and that was where I drew the line at self-congratulation; patting yourself on the back is an unwise thing for a sailor to do.

Still, I was deeply thrilled to be back, and noted a sense of exhilaration at slipping into my chilly bunk, a thrill concentrated by the smell of salty air and seaweed outside, and the scent of dampness that all boats carry. As I dropped off to sleep that night I took comfort from the fact that those inspiring visions of seas and mountains had been won and not given. No one else could see this place exactly the way I did because no one else had arrived here in precisely the same way. Voyaging by sail is travel at its most personal, and even two people on the same boat can claim a wholly different experience.

At midday, two heavily clad blokes clambered over the bulwarks of the old *Micalvi* with the clatter of a boarding party. They dropped their weighty bags on my deck and quickly followed up with their own heavy footfalls. After two weeks with her all to myself, *Wild Song* suddenly felt a little crowded. These were two men I did not really know and had met only briefly in railway station coffee shops: Malcolme in Doncaster on platform 3, and Mike in Paddington just by platform 1.

198

Both were somewhat bemused that a skipper might take on crew after such a brief acquaintance, and so was I.

Mike came recommended, which is always a good sign, but stressed that he was not only seeking an adventure but wanted it to be a learning experience too. He was clocking up miles and knowledge to further his career as a yacht charter skipper. He was in his mid-forties, unattached, had earned his living roughing it with tourists in the Namibian desert, and so I judged he wasn't the sort of bloke to jump ship at the first dollop of cold water, or be distressed if his bunk turned out to be a bit lumpy. He came with the added value of having worked as a chef and had no fear of the stove. For this alone, it was worth the gamble of having him on board. I am usually the galley slave, largely because I am the only one who knows what stores are on board and others cannot always be trusted not to consume the most interesting food first, leaving a dreary prospect as the food lockers slowly empty. I soon appreciated his support when confronting the supermarkets of Puerto Williams, where basics seem plentiful but treats are few and invention is the order of the day. This is when the imaginative cook can really shine. It is too easy for the galley to resort to those plates of stodgy pasta with an insipid red sauce, and call it food.

Then came Malcolme, a Geordie who was smiling from the very start of the trip and who never seemed to lose his grin. I took to him immediately on meeting him when he asked, "Have you got plenty of tools on board? I love it when things go wrong." What more comforting or supportive words could a skipper wish to hear? It's silly to think that nothing will go wrong because it always does, and nothing you can do in your planning is going to prevent it. Things break. You simply have to be well prepared. With an extra man on the job I felt confident that we could overcome most of the mechanical difficulties that small boats throw at you. Malcolme unpacked a navy blue sweater and quickly put it on; it was borrowed from his son who serves in the Royal Navy and it immediately gave the boat a much more professional air. Mike looked more like a backpacker, and I dare say I didn't look much better. Malcolme added class. I warmed to him even more as he unpacked further, asking shyly where he might put his watercolour paints.

The only apparent hint of division between us was over the matter of tea, an issue of great importance on a sailing ship. Mike had gone to the lengths of bringing his own tin mug and said he wanted his tea strong enough to take the enamel off a lavatory pan. Malcolme, on the other hand, had weaker tastes and was happy to have second go at someone's teabag. Mike had sugar, we didn't. Since it is almost a rule whenever I sail that the kettle is hardly ever off the stove, a certain logistical complexity was working its way into the tea-making, and only time and practice would sort it.

Some skippers give not a thought to whether their crew might be enjoying themselves, or getting satisfaction from a trip, but I felt a strong sense that not only did I have to deliver an experience for myself but for them as well. I had, after all, lured them halfway round the world at no small cost. So I sat them down and told them my plan, expressed in such a way that I did not wish to be seen to be laying down the law, more seeking approval. I told them we would *not* go back to Ushuaia, as I had originally intended, because the stores we could buy here were sufficient. To go back to Ushuaia would mean a checking-out procedure here, followed by a check-in there, a quick tour of the shops, check-out Argentina, sail 20 miles, check-in Chile, and we would only be back where we are now having done more check-ins than a Frequent Flyer. They agreed. Then I announced that there were three things on my agenda: an exploration of the Beagle Channel and its glaciers, a sight of Cape Horn if we could manage it, and then 1,200 miles up the south Atlantic back to Piriapolis where they would leave and I would sail on alone. Nods all round. We had made a plan.

We started off well as a team. It's funny how some people just click without any effort while others will never achieve any harmony. Malcolme was dubbed the chief engineer because of his declared love of tools. Mike's job was to watch, learn and fry — except breakfast, which was to become Malcolme's speciality.

We cast off into Sunday morning sunshine and the process began all over again of teaching new crews the ways of the boat, where ropes led, the mistakes to be made, how the reefing worked, how to light the gas and pump the lavatory dry. We edged out of Puerto Williams with the blessing of the Chilean Navy, which had showered many official stamps on much paperwork. Our plan was to head westwards towards the glaciers, and a fresh breeze from ahead sharpened us up and got us in the mood by getting us thoroughly wet, before a failing wind persuaded us to drop the anchor in perfect tranquillity in Caleta Martinez, a cove where the fast ferry from Ushuaia had dropped me a couple of weeks before, and 20 miles west of where we had started. Good progress. We were directly across the water from Ushuaia and could see it clearly, and I felt relief at the thought that I would not have to trudge the waterfront again seeking entrance and departure papers, lingering in a seedy waiting room while they slowly scribbled on form after form with looks on their faces that suggested each page presented a new challenge, even though they had already done this a dozen times that day. I felt sorry for them. Bureaucracy is little more than job creation, and never was work more needed than at this outpost of the world. Yet, do those who are required to do it, those who often have no other choices, do they sense they are engaged in a futile effort and that their life's work is of no matter, other than earning themselves a wage?

For guidance in our navigation we were following the writings of two intrepid and committed Italians, Mariolina Rolfo and Giorgio Ardrizzi, who have written a pilot book of stature, a proper work of literature, an artwork in itself with its carefully crafted and evocative drawings and illustrations. They know what they are talking about, understand every nook and cranny and cleft in the rocks for a thousand miles, and I would ignore them at my peril. My local charts I had bought from the Chilean Navy, but I was well aware that what appears on paper round here does not always coincide with what you see with your eyes, or more importantly with what your GPS tells you. The charts are out, by only a bit, but it is enough to call for concentration.

This first anchorage, at Martinez, was a good example of the difficult decision that must be made when planning to spend a night at anchor in a place where the weather can be uncertain. Many of these safe "holes", these overnight anchorages, are tucked under the shelter of mountains, or in coves with hills and cliffs on three sides. It could blow the strongest hurricane outside but inside the sea might be flat. But that is not the entire picture, for when strong winds blow over the tops of mountains they have a habit of collapsing down the lee side, accelerating as they fall until they arrive on your doorstep and molest you with violence. It would not be unusual for a blast from one of these downdraughts to hit you at 100 knots (well above hurricane strength), but probably for no more than ten seconds or so. Their speed can be such that physical forces cause the winds to spin around themselves like small tornadoes. These williwaws, tripping across the surface of the water like a ballet dancer, leave a mist behind them consisting of the surface water they have sucked up. From the point of view of someone wanting a quiet night, you need to get yourself away from where these winds might strike, and certainly away from any swell or chop that a strong wind might raise.

So you get as close to the shore as you can, which causes you to struggle against your instincts, for usually the greater the distance between boat and land, the better — the two were not meant for each other. Trees can be your saviour. They can give you added shelter, for the wind will whistle over the tops of them leaving you in relative calm. Being close to the shore, though, presents problems, for in a williwaw the wind will blow briefly but strongly from every point of the compass, and at some stage you will be driven towards the land. So you tie yourself in position with long, floating ropes, and put your anchor out ahead so you cannot move in any direction. The gusts might cause your boat to tug at her lines, but you will be secure. All this, of course, was in the realms of theory as far as I was concerned. I was the new boy round here.

In reality it just takes practice, but Mike quickly got the hang of it. He was into the dinghy as soon as the anchor was down, rowing fast and furious to the shore, then clambering over slimy and seaweed-clad rocks. Then came a little cursing, a little knot-tying, then a thumbs-up and we were fast for the night. I looked over the side on that first night and saw through the crystal clear water that the seabed was thick with long, swaying fingers of green kelp, as lush and dense as an underwater rainforest. Malcolme took the bread knife and an old boathook and lashed the two together in readiness for when the anchor came up the next morning, sure to be covered with a rich harvest of tangled greenery.

"I think I will swim in the Beagle Channel," Malcolme announced in sombre tone. We noted his ambition and remarked on the possible water temperature. By the end of the day I noticed he was only adding to his clothing and not removing any. Thanks to Mike's knitting with our vivid yellow ropes (bought what seemed like a thousand years ago in Mar del Plata, and sold by the kilo at a fishermen's chandlery), the night passed undisturbed.

We were now engaged in a circumnavigation of Isla Gordon, a rocky mass 25 miles long and 10 miles at its broadest point. Think of an Isle of Wight but with added fjords, sitting in the middle of the Beagle Channel, dividing it into the south-western and north-western arm. Shivering a little in the cold wind we clipped along, sailing hard but comfortably to windward, cold spray flying and the kettle working overtime producing tea, coffee and Cup-a-Soup as we beat westwards with the north-western arm in sight. The forecast was for 10-knot winds, which turned out to be 25, but the boat shrugged it off and ploughed on, bashing through the chop, fighting not only the headwind but a one-knot current which was against us all the time. We took the first reef in the main and the second shortly after. The staysail remained rolled away as the previous night I had discovered a small tear near the head, and although I had done a hurried repair job this seemed no place to test my needlework to destruction.

The eastern tip of Isla Gordon soon came abeam in sailing conditions no worse than a fresh day in the English Channel. What was all the fuss about? Then, out of the corner of my eye, I caught sight of a heap of white water moving rapidly towards us. It was strung out in a line the full width of the channel as if painted by a linesman's brush. Before I had chance to mentally process this and take action, it was upon us with force. A katabatic wind is one that blows down a mountainside and strikes you from overhead rather than from the side. This means that the more the boat leans over, the more sail is presented to the wind rather than less. So, the katabatic wind, like the bully it is, pins you over ever harder the more you lean away from it. At the very worst you can be laid flat with the possibility of flooding and going under.

"Mainsheet!" I screamed into the roar of the wind and spray. There was hesitation. Neither Mike nor Malcolme had been on board long enough to reach instinctively for the correct line. I grabbed it instead, cracked open the jammer, and then the main was let fly. The boom slammed out to leeward with the sheet whizzing through the blocks and was soon trailing in the water. This is risky, for the weight of the wind in the sail working against the drag in the water can snap it. Mike went quickly to the mast. I let the halyard go from the cockpit, and he grappled the main down till it was smothered. We were still uncomfortably heeled even without the mainsail, and only after deeply reefing the headsail did we regain any kind of control. Needless to say, by the time all this was achieved we had sailed out of that spiteful little band of wind and were hopelessly under-canvassed and dead in the water. It was a warning to go a bit more carefully.

Bahía Yendegaia, the pilot book told me, took its name from an Indian word meaning "deep", and a visiting ship in 1883 reported Yamana Indians living there "miserably dressed having lost the habit of using skins". Bridges (of Harberton) gave them some cattle to enhance their prosperity, and with some success, but as we motored to the head of this placid bay and the blue seawater gave way to a grey, silty outflow from a river, we saw no cattle. Ahead were several wooden ranch houses, and a few buildings that may once have housed livestock. We anchored off the shelving beach as close as we dared and heard dogs bark but saw no people. Horses gathered on the shore, a dozen or more, eyeing us and curious. They became even more inquisitive as we landed in our grey rubber dinghy and hauled it up the beach. We strolled towards them and they took nervous steps towards us, then they skipped quickly past us like naughty schoolchildren and headed straight for the dinghy and gave it the most intensive licking, presumably enjoying the salt. They weren't in the slightest bit interested in us.

This was not an abandoned place at all, despite appearances. The doors of the houses were open and there were signs of life, although we saw no one. Curtains hung from the windows, a quick glance through them showed a kettle and a wood fire, but still no human appeared. We showed respect and didn't venture further. An area behind the house had been fenced off for vegetable growing. It was not clear from the map how you got here other than by sea, nor how you would ever get out again. We spent another gentle night with mountains all around.

Malcolme sang loud and strong the next day, the tunes of joy coming from deep within him. All the way down the Beagle Channel he entertained us with an unstructured number that went, "I am sailing the Beagle Channel ... I am sailing the Beagle Channel ..." And that was it. There was scope for more development but he seemed happy with it as it was. He said his mind was on an epic poem he was going to write about his adventure, but he was having trouble finding enough words to rhyme with Beagle. The sight of him humming away gave me great pleasure, for this experience of voyaging through one of the greatest waterways in the world was too good not to share. Mike brewed Cup-a-Soup again, which became the ship's beverage of choice on these cold days, although it was a brew made something of a gamble because the packets were labelled in Spanish and the picture on the front was not always a true representation of what lay inside.

The outward appearance of the fjords also gave no real clue as to what might be found inside. This is a landscape that often wears a disguise. Bahía Romanche, on Isla Gordon, started off as an undistinguished inlet where, instead of falling straight into the sea, the mountains gave way to gentler slopes where trees grew in the shelter and grass crept nervously over rocks. Here we found a hidden treasure. On the eastern side lay the tightest, narrowest anchorage into which I have ever taken a boat. It was like sailing into a shoe box. We reversed between a vertical rocky cliff having first identified a flat rock — the only clue to the existence of a cleft into which we had to steer. The boat crept backwards slowly, with mercifully no cross winds to drive us off course. Perfectly positioned and feeling rather pleased with myself, I shouted for the anchor to be let go. I listened for that familiar grind of galvanised chain over steel bow roller, but nothing was heard. I gave a little more force and urgency to my order. "It's stuck," Malcolme shouted back. "It won't run."

We were now drifting away from our ideal position and a glance over the side revealed the rocks beneath us were rising and getting closer to the hull. "Get the anchor down, fast!" I shouted, planning to go out and start all over again. "It's still stuck," Malcolme repeated. He and Mike kicked it, swore at it, and just as I was about to give up and start again it finally broke free and rattled to the sea bed. It was not in the perfect spot but it would do. This time we moored with four lines, one from each quarter, for it wouldn't take much shifting of the boat by the wind to have us rubbing up against the rocks on one side or the other. Then it was time to sniff the air, more bracing than any smelling salts. Every breath of wind round here tastes and smells like a fair wind from heaven. I could live on it. Beef and boiled potatoes were feasted upon that night as the chill fell around us. We were alone in the loneliest of places.

The jaw-dropping anchorages now came thick and fast. Just 10 miles to another apparently modest inlet, Seno Pia, on the northern shore. The Beagle was in a misty mood with the grey outlines of distant headlands stacked one behind the other, like cut-out scenery. The sight of it put me on edge for the blackness spoke of threat. We sailed into a dark, misty inlet with openings to either side, like a corridor with doors any one of which might lead to treasure, or trouble. "Watch out for the white stone," the pilot book urged. "You must pass with it on your right!" I had forgotten how to deal with shallows, the water hereabouts generally being 300 chilly metres deep. I motored on. Kelp! Strings of green fingers floating on the surface blocked my way, waving a warning of rocks beneath. I turned away and instead edged towards the western shores before straightening up and bracing myself to make a grand entrance. We were in.

In an instant the wind disappeared, as if a door had slammed shut behind us. Over mirror-like water we edged inland now enclosed by black granite mountains on either side, stunted trees clinging to thin topsoil. Waterfalls fell from above the clouds and were too numerous to count but filled the air with a constant sound of tumbling water.

I felt utter disgust at the sight of a flotilla of what I could only imagine were white polystyrene cups floating on the water ahead. What kind of vandal throws such things overboard here? We gave a collective tut-tut, then were forced to change our minds. No, not plastic cups. Ice! Small lumps of it. The closer we got, the more the white blobs resolved themselves into frozen chunks, jagged and untouched by the weather; others had drifted out of the dark shadows, felt the warm sunshine on their backs and melted into the most intricate shapes, like natural sculptures delicate enough to cradle in your hand. One was a butterfly, another a

210

horse or perhaps a fish. Small though they were, they sent a lurch and a thump through the hull when we occasionally collided, and I backed off the throttle and crept ahead at dead slow.

The air was getting chillier and we shivered, the sky darker as the mountains around us grew ever higher. It was another journey into a wild and unexpected land, our breath held in anticipation. Did revelation lie ahead, or disappointment? The answer was not long in coming. We turned sharply to the right, then straightened up and found ourselves in an inner pool, enclosed where the air was perfectly still, the surface of the water a perfect mirror.

Ahead, a towering wall of ice. A hundred feet high. Its whiteness sparkled, and in the cracks and fissures the light shone deep, electric blue. This was the final thrust of this monumental glacier as it left the land and resigned itself to the sea.

Then a heavy rumble, like thunder ricocheting around the mountains, and we saw an ice boulder the size of a house fall away from the glaciers mass, splintering, cracking, sending waves that rocked us wildly from side to side as they passed under. I killed the engine. The silence was absolute; almost smothering. It was a stillness you could cut with a knife. *Wild Song* slowly lost way and came to a halt. We didn't drop the anchor because there was nothing to move her: no current, no breeze. We stood on the side deck and stared deep into those vivid blue cracks and crevices that scarred the face of the ice, the innermost depths so vivid that they made the eyes ache with their beauty.

211

There was never a bluer blue than this. It was the light of a million years ago. We took to the dinghy and rowed closer to the towering ice wall, not speaking but just taking in the power of it. Small pieces of ice continued to fall from larger blocks and we were mindful that the wash from a hefty fall could swamp us, so we retreated.

Then we looked behind us. There was yet another giant glacier, slithering like a tongue of ice down to the waters of the Beagle. To have glaciers on both sides of your boat is not to be dismissed as an everyday experience and for some time we sat there and drank it all in, supping heartily at the spectacle till we were drunk with it. Then, with the day coming to its end, and with the greatest reluctance, we started the intrusive engine and headed back towards an unnamed anchorage where we spent the night and considered what we had just seen. It was just us, the ice, and the gentle moan of a strengthening wind in the Beagle Channel outside. If there was nothing better in store on this entire voyage, then it would have been worthwhile for this one day alone. With that thought we went early to bed.

After a few nights in some of the most remote anchorages in the whole world, like wandering chicks we felt it was time to be getting back to mother. But first I had to find my way round the western end of Isla Gordon to complete the circuit and get us pointing eastwards again. I chose to ignore the Navy's instruction to use the Canal Thomson, which is wide and safely buoyed, and instead decided to thread my way through the multitude of islands and rocks, saving some 15 miles or more. In the end, it saved nothing whatsoever. I got horribly lost. I was seeking the Canal Barros, a rat-run that would lead me to a narrow channel which, in turn, should take me back to the Beagle proper. Reconciling what I saw with my eyes with what appeared on the chart was difficult. I couldn't fathom it. The GPS was of not much help, and once or twice gave our position as being halfway up a mountainside. We sailed for an hour before I realised we had driven ourselves up a dead end. I am sure Captain Fitzroy aboard the *Beagle* must have muttered, "Oh, bugger," many times in similar situations so I wasn't in bad company. It was dusk by the time we made our retreat and got ourselves on the right road again, grateful for the longer days since this unlit coast was no place to be in the dark. Eventually we regained the Beagle — the south-western arm this time — and could head a few miles east for a night anchorage.

But the Beagle had one more treat to deliver and it took me by surprise. As we emerged from the narrows and into wider water I felt the gentle lift of an ocean swell, the first I had felt for some time. Swell does not make its way into the sheltered waters we had been sailing, so open water, the ocean, must be close. I glanced at the compass to see which direction it was coming from, then at the chart to orientate myself. And then I worked it out.

I had found the Pacific Ocean.

It had been my original intention to sail into the Pacific and head west for many more thousands of miles.

There, at what I thought would be the climax of the voyage, I would find the tiny atoll called Nomwin Atoll that was one of Nicholas's places; a stopping point for *Europa* on her way to Korea. The beauty of the words he used to describe it — "the least loneliest nowhere in the world" — gave the place huge magnetism for me, and his words alone were surely enough to inspire anyone to make the long journey to see for themselves. But somewhere in the vastness of the Atlantic Ocean while heading south, I had decided it was a voyage too far.

From now on, every mile would be one further from home with the prospect of an increasingly lengthy return trip. Nevertheless, if the inspiration had been sufficient, I would have risen to the challenge. But I did not want this to turn into a pilgrimage. It had never been my intention to set out on a whistle-stop tour of the places Nicholas had trodden. What would be the point in that? Better to remember his words of delight at having discovered a place on earth that was his and remained special to *him*. There is no reason any of those places should be special to me simply because he had been there. The joy was his, not mine to try to reproduce. So to remember him best would be by following his example, and not treading in his footsteps or sailing in his wake. I must use my time on unfamiliar seas and in strange lands to find places of my own by invoking his spirit and his courage. That was the only way forward.

I was grateful for that glimpse of the Pacific. I imagined him on it, sailing away.

CHAPTER
SIXTEEN

CAPE HORN

The heat was on when we got back to *Micalvi*. The weather was as balmy as an English summer's day, and we found Denis strolling the deck with his young son, neither wearing sweaters for what must be the first time in months, if not years. This is the sort of place where to turn off your heating is noteworthy, and to sweat is a rare sensation. "Often like this?" I asked, tongue-in-cheek. "About two days a year," said Denis. "Sometimes three."

There was much hustle and bustle across the *Micalvi*'s deck as charter crews left and new ones joined; young people with stuffed rucksacks and damp duffel bags provided a typical quayside scene of hopefuls eager for maritime adventure, and more than a few wearing a look of dread at the prospect. Snapshots of the early stages of adventure have changed little over the years: faces glowing with anticipation or smothered in apprehension.

The warmth of the wind interested me. Prevailing westerly weather hereabouts is fresh and chilly, but a warm wind must have its source elsewhere. I was trying to piece together a picture of what was happening; the weather was up to something. I glanced at the masthead and saw no scudding cloud; the wind was hardly robust enough to be felt on your cheek. It was from the north-east, I also noted, when the usual flow was from the west. Something was up.

At the forefront of my mind was the ambitious business of getting ourselves around Cape Horn. I refused to think of it as "rounding" the Horn for this is properly described as being a passage eastwards or westwards from the latitude 50 degrees south on one side of South America, to 50 degrees south on the other. It is not entirely clear how this definition came about, but the "Cape Horners" make the rules. Now a club, these were once an elite gang who had properly rounded the Horn under sail, often enduring great hardship and struggle in the days of square-rigged ships. These days the membership seems mostly drawn from participants in round-the-world ocean races and perhaps a few long-distance cruisers.

Sailors like me, on the other hand, who want to take a look at Cape Horn the easy way, are able to leave from *Micalvi* before breakfast and, under the right conditions, have sailed round the Horn before the next dawn and be well on our way back by lunchtime the next day. It almost falls into the "day trip" kind of sailing. Quite rightly, the Cape Horners wanted to differentiate between the two kinds of "rounding". So I had no plans in my mind of "rounding the Horn" but to sail "around it" was our honest intention — it is, after all, an island. It would be disrespectful, anyway, to make any great claim for my short sprint. I was aware of those thousands who had given their lives in the past to achieve it. The literature of the time overflows with tales that make your heart miss a beat with images of towering seas, exhausted crews, appalling food and whipping winds. All these horrors drip from the pages. So Cape Horn I did not see as an attraction, rather a memorial to be visited with respect, and not merely gawped at.

But when should we go? We were not the only boat alongside *Micalvi* who had their eyes on this trophy. Several were keenly watching the weather forecast, but shaking their heads. "Not this week," most agreed. A stout but small German steel yacht beside us had consulted the forecasts, written off the next seven days as a possibility and decided to go hillwalking instead. A boat skippered by a New Zealand lawyer was going to head off and see what they could make of it but he wasn't hopeful. In the interests of managing expectations, I told my crew that it was unlikely we would get round, but we would have a go.

As we clambered across the boats that evening after supper, heading for the bar, I glanced up at the masthead again, as was now becoming my habit, and saw the wind still light and from the east. Surely, this could not last. As I settled into my favourite seat by the *Micalvi*'s log burner, I glanced through a brass scuttle and saw how unusually still the waters of the Beagle Channel had become. Strange how such stillness can give rise to stirring thoughts. A plan was forming in my mind, and a somewhat risky one.

217

With the wind unchanged the following morning, like the grand old Duke of York I marched right up to the top of the hill to confront the Chilean Navy with my plan, which they must approve before I was allowed to leave. It is largely a matter of routine, but routine matters more than most things round here. When I had satisfied them that I had 150 litres of diesel aboard and food for three weeks, the rubber stamp fell heavily on yet another lengthy document and I was free to sail for Cape Horn, with a warning that I must stick to the route they had outlined. The Chilean Navy operate with such charm that it is difficult to begrudge them their paperwork, for they clearly enjoy it so much.

Although I had shared my plan with the authorities, I did not discuss it with the crew. Quite the reverse: I lied to them as to my intentions. I suggested we would "go and have a look" and "there's not much chance, but we'll see". In fact, I told them we were heading for Puerto Toro that night, a convenient harbour at the eastern end of Navarino Island, and a good place to wait for the right weather. My abiding suspicion, however, was that the right weather was already upon us. For the moment, I decided to keep that thought to myself.

If you were God and wanted to create the nastiest little corner in the world, then you couldn't do better than create Cape Horn. If you begin at the Horn and circle the world, you will arrive back where you started having crossed no land mass. The waves and currents created by the prevailing westerly wind, in turn created by the spinning of the earth, are well aware of this, and

218

so the unstoppable rollers thunder around the globe at this latitude unimpeded. To make things worse, some 600 miles to the south of Cape Horn lies the Antarctic peninsula, which narrows their pathway. As far as the waves and swells are concerned it is like three motorway lanes suddenly reducing to one, and we know the chaos and confusion when that happens. But cars have little momentum compared to waves and so traffic will grind to a halt, but waves and swells will heap upon each other as the leaders are slowed and the ones behind catch up. This causes dangerous confusion. To add even more spice to this recipe, the seabed south of Cape Horn rises, so the confusion is amplified in more than one plane. Then comes the relentless westerly wind that blows off the Pacific Ocean, first meeting the high Andes where, rather than make the effort to rise above them, they bounce off and are deflected south. So, a disturbed ocean is whisked up into even more of a frenzy by a frustrated wind. Add to this the temperamental nature of the low pressure systems that barrel through here bringing sudden and violent shifts in the wind, and you have the perfect recipe for a nasty little place.

This was why an easterly wind intrigued me so much. Surely, if the wind had been from this direction for a couple of days then several angry forces were no longer able to play a part. Certainly there would be no locally created swell, which can reach overwhelming heights. It was crazily possible we might get round in a flat calm!

We motored eastwards along the Beagle Channel that afternoon, helped by that knot of perpetual current which ran now in our favour, then turned slowly to the right to follow the pine-clad coast of the island. The sun was beginning to drop behind the mountains of Navarino, the sea was perfectly flat, and there was not enough wind to fill the sails. It seemed crazy not to go for it, stupid not to try for the Horn that night and get it in the bag. It might be our last chance. The only contradictory thought in my mind was the weather forecast, which hitherto had seemed uncannily accurate round here. It had spoken of strong westerly winds, well above 35 knots. That is what had kept the other skippers alongside. Why should I be right and they be wrong? I had to make a decision.

I throttled back so that what I said could be heard clearly. "Gentlemen," I declared, "We are going to stand on." I was met with a blank look from both Malcolme and Mike. I don't think they had heard the expression before. "We're going to go for the Horn tonight," I explained, and then outlined my thinking. The night would be short and daylight would be arriving by the time the navigation was at its trickiest, for there would have to be a certain amount of eyeball navigation given that the charts hereabouts do not always agree with the GPS. There was one navigation light on the entire route marking a dangerous rock, but if we found it and identified it we would be OK. I said it was possible that the weather would break without warning and we might have to turn back as so many had done before, so hopes should not be allowed to rise too high. I sent Mike off to the stove to prepare some belly-filling grub. It was going to be a concentrated night.

With Navarino Island astern of us we were now crossing the open water of Bahía Nassau, which would leave us exposed until we gained some shelter from the Wollaston Islands. Shelter was not needed that night, though. All that was required of us was to gaze at the vivid sunset that cast the islands into sharp relief, enjoy the gentle dissolve of daylight into night and savour the salty taste of the fine mist that fell around us. This large, open bay was flat and peaceful with not a hint of temper about it. We were well aware, however, that these places can behave like a sleeping tiger, and all that was needed was for us to tread on its tail and all hell could break loose — this thought unspoken, but in the backs of our minds. We pressed on.

The lads took it in turns to rest, although I suggested they did so in their oilskins in case they were suddenly needed. Perhaps I was being over-cautious. A breeze would have been welcome to give us a sail towards the Horn. How crazy to be sailing for Cape Horn and hoping for more wind. I didn't rest. I navigated myself into the ground, taking bearings, getting fixes, reading the pilot book to make sure that my escape plan was ready if conditions should turn for the worse. It was a chilly night. Mugs of hot soup were called for on a regular basis.

There is one big decision to make in approaching Cape Horn from the north, and for hours I could not make up my mind. To the north of Isla Hornos lie Isla

Herschel and Isla Deceit, with passages between them and also to the north of them, and to the west of Herschel. In other words, there are two routes down to the Horn. But which to choose? If I chose the Canal Franklin and sailed to the western tip of Herschel, I was then 5 miles west of the Horn and could bear away and enjoy a fast ride down to and eventually round it. That was a strong option. But Canal Franklin is wide open to the west and I would be staring directly into the face of the Pacific Ocean throwing its waves and swells at me. It is here, in this short stretch of troubled water, that many are defeated and forced to turn back. The pilot book warns, sternly, that progress through here against wind and swell can be impossible. But if you make it you have cracked it and the Horn is yours, which makes it a tempting prospect.

An alternative is to pass between Herschel and Deceit through the Paso Mar del Sur, avoiding a rocky, low island in the middle which carries a warning light. This brings you directly to the backside of Isla Hornos and a mere 10-mile beat will have you off its western tip ready to bear away for the Horn itself. Although a 10-mile sail into the wind does not sound a lot, this can quickly become a sail too far. Although there is land on three sides of you, you are exposed from the worst possible direction, which is the west. I pondered this for hours and opted for the latter route. It's shorter and I sensed time was against us. It was as simple as that.

The night was at its blackest as we started to feel the islands close around us, and it was still pitch black as we felt our way into relative safety in the lee of

Wollaston and Herschel. A slight lifting of the sky from black to dark grey spoke of dawn and with it would come some welcome visibility. We strained our eyes to try to make out a light beacon on the rock in the middle of Paso Mar del Sur, and were more than relieved to spot this feeble flickering bulb, for it reassured us that we were exactly where we thought we were. Having been lost once already in the western end of the Beagle Channel, I knew how easy it was to deceive yourself by wishful navigation in these parts.

There was much joy as we raised that dim navigation light, although by now there was just enough light to see what we were trying to avoid and it looked a nasty piece of work. A breeze came in from the west and it was time to set sail. Broad daylight now and we emerged from between the islands and saw the barren north-eastern face of Isla Hornos. The old bugger was nearly within our grasp.

But what a desolate sight this bleak rock landscape was. There were no trees, and no vegetation more than an inch high. I doubt that wind alone has the force to smooth the surface of granite, but the islands looked as though they had been subject to unrelenting shaping by the elements since the dawn of time. Our course was now towards the south-west. Ominously, it was from that direction that the wind started to blow.

It came gently at first, enough to fill the sails and give us 4 knots, but built quickly till the first reef was pulled down, then the second. The headsail was quickly reefed and then the staysail, till we were flying not short of storm canvas and *Wild Song* looked like she had had her clothes hastily ripped from her. The Horn was within reach but not yet in our grasp. It could so easily slip away.

This was, without doubt, the most desolate stretch of water I have ever sailed. The barren rocks to the north gave no comfort, and in the landscape there was little pleasure. Rocky pinnacles off Isla Hornos spoke only of threat. The sky was lowering and the wind now had a moan to it. The spray was flying, cold and sharp on the face. I had not slept and didn't have the strength for a battle, and became less than enthusiastic when it became clear we would not get through on one tack. There was not much sense of relaxation here, it was not a place to sit and gawp, and something about it eclipsed any sense of adventure. Only a sense of survival remained. I wanted to get this over with.

Inch by inch we got to the western tip of Isla Hornos and the temptation to bear away to make the ride smoother was overwhelming, yet a sense that to do so too early might create more problems than it solved prevented me from turning the wheel. Then, once it was clear that we were going to get a clear run down to the Horn and not a moment before, I did make the turn to let her fly over the turbulent, crested sea whipped into spiky water by the advancing Pacific waves meeting the reflections that bounced back from the cliff faces. She raced now, unhindered by wave or spray. Great dollops of the icy green water raced aft along the side decks and dropped themselves into the cockpit, but we didn't care. We were running fast and free, for the Horn.

224

I glanced at the compass. "Hey, we're heading east," I cried. "We must be round!" Amazingly, it was difficult to be certain. We nearly sailed round Cape Horn without realising it, which is easier to do than you might think. "There's the first lighthouse," I shouted, pointing to a lonely modest lantern perched high on the rocks. There are two lights on Cape Horn and this was the most southerly. "We're round," I declared. "Well, bugger me," said Malcolme. "Our skipper's got us round the Horn!" There was cheering, there were photographs, and then there were unexpected rocks ahead and I made a quick alteration of course to seaward, at the same time reminding myself of where I was and that I had to pay more attention. Malcolme was later to point out that he'd seen many pictures of yachts rounding Cape Horn but he'd never seen one as close as we had come.

And then it was all over and we were pointing north-east.

Malcolme pulled the sea-soaked blue woolly hat from his head and announced, "I shall never, ever wash this hat. It's got Cape Horn salt on it!"

If ever there was a song to sing, it was the one wild song that filled all our heads at that moment.

CHAPTER
SEVENTEEN

BENEATH THE
SOUTHERN CROSS

Cape Horn was at a turning point, and as I stared at the most southerly headland in the world I thought what greater and more symbolic turning point could one lifetime have?

The focus was now on returning home, which I knew was potentially the greatest challenge of the voyage. Wind and weather had, by and large, treated me kindly. It would not be fair to expect good fortune to follow for all the 9,000 miles to home.

Back at *Micalvi*, deeply satisfied with ourselves but not showing it, we did the rounds of the Puerto Williams shops yet again. We shuffled our way through the shanty-town shopping centre with our carrier bags, trying to guess if we had food for three weeks; we came to terms with the tragic discovery that instant soup was in short supply and only came in asparagus flavour.

The passage itself as far as Piriapolis, where Malcolme and Mike would leave, was 1,200 miles, and given that "windless" is a word hardly ever used in connection with that stretch of water, we reckoned to allow a fortnight. We filled the tank to the brim with diesel, topped up the water tanks, checked the rigging screws and every other bit of kit we could think of. I had a growing sense that after nearly 10,000 miles the old boat was beginning to feel a little weary; if I was developing aches and pains from the exertion, it would be surprising if she didn't feel the strain too. When things are rough, I can sit in the cockpit imagining what might break next, and how would I deal with it. It's not a depressing process. Once you have thought such things through and decided you could cope, a great sense of relaxation takes over. To have confronted problems before they occur is empowering. However, I was sufficiently aware of the tricks of fate, and knew that the things that go wrong are never the ones you prepare for.

We spent several days as prisoners of both the wind and the Chilean Navy. When wind speeds reach 25 knots, a flag goes up and the Navy declares the harbour closed. Until the flag is down no paperwork will be stamped. This was a testing time. We were anxious to get away.

Then, in the evening, the wind started to drop. Excitement and anticipation started to boil over. But as dusk fell the prison flag, although hanging limp, still showed from the Navy's stately white mast. We were going to be here for yet another night. With dawn came a hurried stamping of paperwork, and we were off. While Mike and Malcolme scurried around making ropes into coils and stowing them, I went to the radio to inform the harbour control of our departure.

When I had finished my conversation, I heard a call on the radio that brought me up short. It was *Europa* — Nicholas's old ship. I knew she had been around Ushuaia to load passengers for an Antarctic trip, but didn't dare hope that I might see her. She meant so much to me and to hear her calling out, if only on the radio, was to bring me close to tears. From her overheard conversation with the Argentine coastguard I had figured her whereabouts and strained to see her in the mist ahead. She was roughly 5 miles ahead of us but the visibility was frustratingly less than that. How I craved to see her, not only for a sight of that beautiful ship set in the perfect frame of the Beagle Channel, but because by having contact with her I was also close to the spirit of Nicholas, which must surely cling to her decks and in her rigging. I could not have been more excited if I had known he was alive and well and sailing ahead of me, out of sight.

She kept herself hidden for another hour and although I kept the thought to myself, I spent many of those minutes staring into the murk. Even with binoculars I couldn't make her out. I resigned myself to not seeing her, certain that the glimpse of her I craved would not happen. But happen it did, just when I had started to put her from my mind. Her stately, dignified and overpowering outline turned from a fuzzy smudge on the horizon into her unmistakable and beautiful shape. I now faced the entire Atlantic Ocean with more courage than I had felt for some time, because of her.

★ ★ ★

I looked over my shoulder for one last view of the Beagle Channel. It had lost none of its magic. It remained one of the most inspiring vistas of my life, although I find it difficult to be certain why. I was sailing with so many unanswered questions. I saw the distant islands making stepping stones down to Cape Horn, and they still frightened me. There were so many places, so many sights I wanted to pay my respects to — places I would never see again.

To the future I had to look, though, and with some effort I turned my head forward. We had to hit the Le Maire Strait, between Staten Island and Tierra del Fuego, at slack water when the racing tide was not flowing, which I calculated to be about two in the morning. Having come through it unscathed while heading southbound, I wasn't going to let it get one up on me now. With a combination of the sails and a little breeze, and the engine to keep us going through the calms, we made our way slowly eastwards. With the help of the east-going current we quickly ticked off the bays and headlands that had proved so troublesome some months before. We were on an eastbound escalator, riding it fast and easy.

We entered the south Atlantic proper, north of Staten Island, at about three in the morning. I felt the moment sharply. As we came out of the lee of Tierra del Fuego we took a steep sea on the beam, which raced along the deck and found its way down the hatch directly above my bunk, soaking it. Goodbye, Beagle Channel.

A westerly blast was no reason for disappointment. We were in the Furious Fifties and the Roaring Forties were several hundred miles ahead, with the expected lighter weather a few hundred miles further still. If you can't get a decent westerly blow round Staten Island, where are you going to get one? However, I have read enough accounts by others to know that "prevailing winds never prevail" — to quote the words of Blondie Hasler, one of the great singlehanded sailors of the twentieth century. I wanted to get the next 400 miles over with as quickly as possible; getting ourselves north of Puerto Deseado, at roughly 48 degrees south, would be a major hurdle behind us. After that I would feel safer. It is purely psychological, of course, but it seems helpful to break a long passage with mileposts.

It was rough ride up to Deseado and at one point we hove to for several hours for a short-lived gale to blow through. Then it was back to big seas, strong winds on the beam, ceaseless green water across the decks and difficult living when the act of standing up below decks was not a task to be taken lightly. The galley maintained a decent performance and Malcolme served up the cooked breakfasts without complaint or interruption, even on one occasion passing me my bacon sandwich to devour while still in my bunk. I took good advantage of this, knowing that singlehanders cannot possibly enjoy such a luxury and I had some lonely months ahead.

I found it a nervous ride north. I felt that luck had been very much on my side so far, and luck eventually runs out. I often quoted my old granny, a woman with

230

glum Yorkshire blood flowing in her veins and consequent bleak outlook on life, who never missed an opportunity to remind us that bad times were always just around the corner. The moment any pleasure crossed our path she would intone, "We'll pay the price for this." And so I crept northwards forever under the cloud of her dark prophecy. For the first time I felt uneasy in my bunk on the port quarter, underneath the cockpit seats. With the boat well heeled to port I could clearly hear the water rushing past the hull, and became conscious that only a thin skin of plastic kept us apart. When the seas started to break over the bow and run aft, I also sensed water above me and it started to feel far too much like a watery grave. The GPS, at one point, started to lose its position and gave a pathetic warble of an alarm, like a child that had his lost its mother. It wasn't significant, but it puts you on edge. Then came a poor forecast of strong north-westerly winds, and the discovery of a once dry locker now dripping with seawater, and the instruments showing a relentless rise in the wind strength. One little thing after another led to a deep craving to be safe in Piriapolis and have this leg of the voyage done. I needed to find a more confident frame of mind to carry me up the Atlantic Ocean.

Then came another alarm, this time from the AIS, which stands for Automatic Identification System, and is a radio receiver which decodes transmission from nearby ships. These radio signals tell you the vessel's position, its speed and its course. It is also fed with information from your own GPS and so it is able to compute with deadly accuracy how close a ship will come, at what time that will be, and give an alarm if there is a risk of collision. This is all presented on a small screen in a user-friendly way. Of all the things the GPS revolution has given us, I believe this to be the greatest with regard to safety of yachts at sea. In times past, to determine whether a ship was on a collision course, you took out your hand-held compass and recorded a series of bearings. If they did not change, you were in trouble. Now that is all done for you by microchip. It has the advantage over the compass of being available in poor visibility, and of warning you well in advance of arising situations. The downside is that it makes you idle and less in tune with all around you, as all yacht electronics do. In the case of AIS I think it is a decent trade-off.

For much of the voyage so far the AIS had had an easy time, with so few ships seen and none of those posing any threat. So it was with some surprise, when about a hundred miles offshore, that I saw the poor little thing come to life and display no fewer than thirty close-packed targets. Out here, in this great nowhere? It must be a fault. We examined the targets one by one. They showed every one of the ships as being at anchor. But this was the open ocean and we were 200 miles offshore. It didn't seem possible. Soon the fleet of which the AIS had warned came into view, and what a depressing sight it was.

These were gigantic factory ships, swaggering bullies anchored in 100 metres of water on a convenient bank several hundred miles offshore. Their job was the premeditated raping of the seas. They rose and fell to a long, low swell that had the rhythm of a dinosaur's slumbering breath; each revealing their underwater vastness as the swells rolled under them. On the VHF radio we heard the occasional babbling oriental voices. These were squid hunters who anchored by day and fished after dark, luring vast quantities of squid by the use of bright lights and nets. This is home to *Illex argentinus*, one of the most important commercial squid species in the world. The annual catch in the last decade of the twentieth century was over 100,000 tons. They spawn further north than here and are carried south on the warm Brazilian current until they meet the northbound and chilly Falklands current in which we were now sitting. Here they flourish. And so do the ships. So valuable is this catch that it forms the basis of yet another dispute between Britain and Argentina in the squid-rich waters around the Falkland Islands. I like squid, but I didn't like the look of this lot. Armed with both technology and sheer brute force, here was yet another eco-disaster in the making. What nasty pieces of work those big ships looked. How glad I was to leave them astern.

Slowly the wind became less forceful as the latitude decreased, and became warmer. We were soon able to rid ourselves of the first sweater, then the second, and by the time we were level with the Valdes Peninsula we felt we had emerged into a different world of warmth and sunshine. Of course, there was still the unpredictable River Plate ahead where deadly pamperos and sudestadas can form. These are areas of strong wind bred on the inland pampas and fuelled by the warmth of sea as they track eastwards, making for malicious little weather systems. But my weather downloads showed only light headwinds and we spent several impatient days on flat seas making less progress than we would have liked with the wind from ahead.

Mike gave us a lecture on the stars of the southern hemisphere and I remember feeling the sheer power of the Southern Cross, which I would stare at for hours. It is a simple yet mesmerising constellation. It was now noticeably lower in the sky than I remembered it from when we were further south, so we were making progress. With several hundred miles to go, the wind became frustratingly light but we were able to enjoy the gentle sway of the mast as it fingered its way across a vivid Milky Way. We could all sleep easily and with comfort, and with the boat upright for most of the time, invention returned to the galley. There were moments of great harmony when the set of the sails and the rise and fall of the boat to the waves seemed in perfect tune, singing their own wild song.

CHAPTER
EIGHTEEN

THE LONG HAUL
NORTH

It had been six months since I was last in Piriapolis, nervously fitting out for the big leg south, and now that was behind me and soon I would be doing the same again, this time for the long leg northwards towards home. It was a different challenge, but no less testing.

We approached in the early evening and I gazed shorewards and spotted the chandlery where a dour but helpful man does his best with limited stock. I could see what I remembered as a deserted beach, but now packed with evening strollers and bathers. The air crackled with the sound of wood fires and the scents of cooking food. It was barbecue season. It is amazing how strong a bond a sailor forms with a harbour that has once given him comfort and shelter. This felt like the next best place to home.

It was here that I bid a somewhat sad farewell to Mike and Malcolme. I was sorry to see them walking away from the boat, hauling their heavy kit bags behind them, bound for the airport. Both had been as good a crew as you could wish for: willing, capable, good company. Malcolme said to me as he left, "Don't set off yet. Wait till you're busting to go." He was a singlehander and well understood how daunting was the prospect of a 6,000-mile solo sail. At that moment, "busting to go" was the very last emotion in me. I needed some rest, not to regain physical strength but to achieve the necessary frame of mind, which must be one of resilience and optimism. An outlook that was less than 100 per cent positive was going to erode to nothing long before the passage was done. I wanted to make a creditable attempt at it, and for that I had to be clear in my head what it was really all about.

I spent a lot of time walking around town, just thinking, and had many low moments at the prospect of what lay ahead. It was unlikely to be an easy passage; certainly there would be little of that gentle downwind drifting that had wafted me south. I would have to fight my way north; there was no free ticket for this ride.

The preparation began. I thought a week would be long enough and it was in fact eight days before I left. But every moment of those days was filled with hauling heavy shopping the mile from the supermarket to the boat, then re-stowing, fixing, checking, and eventually sleeping. Thankfully, a forecast of strong winds kept me in harbour for an extra couple of days. I was grateful for that, because I had promised myself that I would be blindly accepting of whatever the ocean threw at me en-route and not grumble, but I was damned well going to make an easy start of it, and at a time to suit myself when I felt ready to ease into the routine of being alone again at sea.

With the boat stowed, gas bottles filled, and all the other little details attended to, I eventually found myself in that "busting to go" frame of mind Malcolme had recommended, and rather grandly filed my passage plan by phone to Falmouth Coastguard in the UK, advising them "singlehanded to Falmouth UK. ETA 80 days." Once that message had been sent, a new and forward-looking attitude took hold, which I hoped would see me through a totally new adventure.

Libby and I spoke often on the phone. I remembered some words of encouragement she had offered to a friend of ours who found himself in a difficult place and she recited it off the top of her head. It was from the Anglo Saxon poem "The Battle of Maldon":

Let the heart be stronger, the courage greater, spirit the higher, as the strength grows less.

That so appealed to me that I was tempted to take a chisel and carve it across the bulkhead so that its empowering thought should never leave my gaze. Then she confounded me with an even better one, perfectly suited to the moment, and a sharp reminder to someone who had once, in a rather cowardly way, made vague enquiries about having his boat put on the deck of a big ship and brought back to England the easy way.

There must be a beginning of any great matter, but the continuing unto the end until it be thoroughly finished yields the true glory.
— Sir Francis Drake

With dusk falling and the lights of ships at anchor in the River Plate beginning to twinkle in the distance, and with the flashing of the navigation marks to guide me outwards, I set off into the south Atlantic. I said farewell to Piriapolis for the last time. The sea was lumpy — in the way that estuary seas always are — due to two days of strong winds, and with the breeze light I made little progress that night, motoring to get away from the bustle of Punta del Este and into the less cluttered safety of the open sea. The first night was tiring. I was out of the habit of sailing alone. The AIS was hardly ever silent as inward and outbound ships appeared one after the other in procession, and I found myself short-tacking along the shore, which was something I promised myself I would not do. The alternative was to be on a south-easterly tack, which would mean pointing at South Africa and sailing ever further from home. At the start of this lengthy passage, that thought was too much to bear.

I soon got back into my solo-sailor's sleep routine which, in crowded waters, is the one that consists of slumbering in twenty-minute stretches followed by a quick look around, then back to sleep again for another twenty. I thought such a regime would be torture, but when I first tried it on the transatlantic race in 2005 I found it surprisingly refreshing. That night the moon shone clear and full in the sky, beaming through the cabin windows. I sang to myself a silly song, an American nursery rhyme remembered from childhood, "I See the Moon". Libby tells me that when I am away,

238

she sometimes looks to the moon and sings it also. Perhaps she was doing so at that very moment.

By breakfast time I felt comfortably alone and on my way. There was nothing to be seen, and I tacked, having set the lightweight genoa to try to catch some breeze. By lunchtime I was surprised to see the coast off La Paloma dead ahead: in my mind I had said my goodbyes to the South American landmass and didn't expect to see it again.

I had divided the passage into legs because I found it easier to get a mental grasp on it that way, and only when one leg was over would I think about the next. The first push was to the latitude of Rio de Janeiro at about 22 degrees south — a thousand miles away. By then I should be several hundred miles out into the Atlantic and should pick up an easterly wind, providing the weather was acting according to past form, which is always a gamble. From there the next leg would be to the equator, a further 1,400 miles. Of the entire passage, this should be the easiest leg, for I would have a reaching wind in an area of famously benign weather. North of the equator I would pay the price, as the doldrums would have to be crossed. Then the north-east trades would kick in and take me up to the Azores, where the westerly winds would then blow me home. How the Gods of Sea and Weather were to make a complete fool of me.

With those unexpected tower blocks of La Paloma in sight, I took my chance and grabbed a wind forecast via my mobile phone — a facility Fitzroy and the *Beagle* could never have imagined and about which I felt ridiculously guilty. It showed three days of fair and strong south-westerly winds. This seemed too great a blessing even to have wished for. It arrived as forecast, and with the wind astern we sped along at 6 lovely knots with just a scrap of jib to catch the force six breeze, aiming for 20S, 30W, which seemed to be the point at which an easterly or south-easterly might be expected. Over the days the seas grew until substantial swells were rolling up behind us. I cannot explain why I held my breath at the sight of every single one of them, for I was pretty confident by now that this boat would float over them. Even so, I was not sufficiently relaxed to enjoy the sight of mighty south Atlantic swells lifting us high on to their peaks and dropping us deep into the valleys, each one reminding me how easily we could be toyed with. To add to the nervousness, after a hurried repair back in Piriapolis the masthead light failed again, which was no real cause for concern because I could set the anchor light swinging from the backstay. Nor did I expect much traffic, and in fact I was not to see another ship till almost on the equator.

Shortly after the failure of the navigation light, I noticed severe chafing to the self-steering lines, which connect the wind vane to the wheel. With much stretching and bending and hanging over the back of the boat, I was able to replace them. I remember this as a time when I started to spend long periods below. The sun was getting increasingly strong as we made our way north and there was too much wind to set the cockpit awning, so I retreated for much of the day into my shady bubble, coming out towards evening to enjoy that lovely moment when the sun sets and it feels as if someone has shut the oven door.

Deck jobs were growing increasingly urgent but I was going to have to wait until the water was flatter before tackling them. With frequent gusts of 35 knots between the showers and with much water sluicing along the decks, I knew I might be waiting some time. Also, the damned anchor was rattling in the bow fairlead and sent a heavy metallic clang through the hull at the rise of every wave, making the place sound like a breaker's yard. Glancing up at the mainsail, I noticed the sail itself had become detached from one of the slides that hold it to the mast. Just one makes no difference, but breakages like these seem infectious, and if one has parted who is to say others will not follow? The eight cans of diesel lashed to the guardrails had come loose and needed re-lashing otherwise they would be over the side when I wasn't looking.

After all this time I had spent at sea, you might expect me to no longer have any fear of it, but I still found the sight of it unnerving. It is the top curl of a following wave that makes me shudder: the white frothy bit that spits itself into the cockpit and along the side decks, reminding you that the sea can take you any time it wants. You are playing a game with it, and God has given you a decent hand by providing you with a little ship that sails strong and true, but a game it remains and with it comes the possibility of losing. I worried a lot about the engineering of it all. How can all this wire, all these ropes, nuts, bolts and cloth stand up to this repeated nagging by the sea? Why does it all hold together? Who makes it so? Unable to answer these questions to my own satisfaction, I made a habit of reefing early whenever there was a rise in the wind. I never pushed the boat to her limits; my threshold arrived much sooner than hers. As for the motion, by day six I was getting pretty weary of it: the hanging on, the lurching, the reaching and grabbing, and I started to long for the flatter waters that I remembered on the way south.

Of course, when the inevitable calm did arrive, on day seven, I quickly became very cross about it. All I needed was a couple of hours of flat water to get jobs done, but when the hours stretched beyond twenty-four I started to get impatient. To pass the time, I spent a lot of effort getting rid of a fishy odour caused by an unfortunate squid getting caught between the dancing jerry cans of diesel on deck, and then squashed. But when that had been cleared, and the anchor lashed and sail reattached to the mast, I found myself still being bounced around in leftover swell but making no progress. Although I was tired, the motion was too great to allow sleep, so I started the engine and motored ahead at low revs, just to quieten things down a bit. I knew it was a bit early in the passage for an indulgence like this, and I knew it was a habit I must not cultivate.

Towards the end of that period of discomfort came one of the best moments of the passage so far. I have often noticed how, after some kind of testing time at sea, a vivid atmosphere descends: what might be called a moment of revelation when the sea seems more beautiful than you have ever seen it before, a sense of new appreciation overtakes you and fear dissipates. The sea is being revealed to you in its perfect Platonic form. Perceptions are heightened. The motion of the boat, which had once irritated you, now has a classical balletic feel; the blueness of the sky is dazzling not only to your eyes but stirring to the spirit also. The isolation has a heightened yet unthreatening intensity. It is a moment of perfection, and the feeling of self-contentment is huge.

Only an isolated bleep from the AIS broke the magic. It warned of a ship not far away, although the bleeping did not last for long and it may well have been interference from some onboard source. Those bleeps amused me. It was like picking up futile signals from a distant civilisation trying to get in touch, but with no means of replying. The bleeps came like voices from the other side, heard but source unseen. I ignored them.

After a day of calm, the wind came from a new direction. I was fearing it would be a north-easter and I would have a beat on my hands all the 1,000 miles to my waypoint east of Rio, but obligingly it was from the north, so I hauled in the sheets and we romped along, hard on the wind, spray flying, making good progress. The wind was coming in gusts and strengthening, and I remember that as a night when I had little sleep as I reefed and unreefed to keep her going in building seas. Then the wind swung into the dreaded north-east and I crossly went to my bunk at 3am and left her to sort herself out. She was now heading on a disappointing west of north.

The problem with a wind shift is that for the first few hours after the wind has changed direction, the sea and the waves have not yet succumbed, and so we were sailing headlong into an old swell, rising to it and falling off the far side with a crack that at times sounded as if the boat might be about to split open. The sea is a bit like an old works manager who doesn't like "new ways of doing things," so it drags its feet and makes the wind wait till it is ready to march to its tune. Everything jarred. It was impossible to relax in my bunk, tins jumped in their lockers, the kettle bounced its way across the stove. Worse, it was slowing us down. It was breakfast time before normal service was resumed, but by then the force six wind was raising a decent sea of its own and so we continued to crash along, and did so for another ten days.

The fresh food was lasting far better than I thought, in particular the potatoes and the tomatoes, and together with a fried onion and some added protein (canned fish or a fried egg) made for enjoyable suppers. I grew to like the evenings best and soon got into a satisfying routine. At about six I would hang the anchor light from the backstay and plug it in. Then I would start the food preparation, peeling potatoes and onions, trying to make it last as long as possible. This was done to the accompaniment of the BBC World Service, which had an excellent news magazine at this time of day. I was to learn much about the election of a new pope, and more about the life of Margaret Thatcher, who died while I was at sea, than ever I would have done had I been at home.

I tried not to eat before seven, not wanting to make the night seem even longer, but as soon as the seven o'clock pips passed I would wedge myself on the companionway steps, sometimes with a cushion and under the protection of the spray hood, and I would eat. By the time I had finished it would be dark, and when the washing-up was done I would sit in the cockpit (if the going was dry) and simply drink in the night sky. I had a strong sense that I would never see this south Atlantic sky again from the deck of my own boat, and took every chance to marvel at it and get to know its stars. It was deeply satisfying to derive a sense of the direction not by looking at sterile instrumentation but by the presence of the great Southern Cross hovering over my right shoulder. I sat for hours at a time in the warm breeze, completely star struck. But the moment is easily broken by prosaic thoughts. I remember becoming convinced that I did not have sufficient tea bags and dived to the chart table to make speed/distance and tea-consumption calculations, which proved there was no problem, yet.

After days of rough seas and hard on the wind, a sharp afternoon deluge of rain brought with it a failing north wind and a flatter sea. I swear I could smell Brazil, now several hundred miles to the north. The air had an earthy rather than a salty scent. It spoke of greenery, vegetation and rainforest. Not ocean. The boat felt dead that evening, although I didn't miss the wild motion of the days gone by. I was now a quarter of the way home and felt a new weather system taking charge and a new phase of the voyage beginning. It was time to try to set aside the frustrations so far and savour all that nature was surrounding me with. This unique experience in my life was fast ebbing away; at times this voyage felt as though it would last for ever, and at others that it would all too soon be over. I heard the deep sigh that the boat gives as she rises and falls, caused by her bow cutting the swells. She sounds as if she is taking a breath. Sighing at me, perhaps.

One night remains vivid in my mind. For a moment I switched off the lonely little light dangling from the backstay and it seemed we floated in space, not on the sea. There was no visible line of demarcation between sea and sky; the two blended seamlessly. In fact, so clear was the reflection of the brighter stars as the water flattened that it was possible to believe you were floating amongst the stars. And far from feeling a lonely, futile figure in the midst of a universe, I felt as large as anything around me, and only when the cockpit light went back on did I reveal myself and shrink into my true insignificance. While I had been away, Libby had been preparing a radio play based on Nicholas's book, *The Silence at the Song's End*. I was unable to make any contribution, or even act as a sounding board, although I had total faith in her judgement and she in turn had great confidence in her producer. That afternoon it was transmitted and Libby sent me a text message via satellite to tell me it had been a huge success. She was showered with emails, book sales were storming ahead, his flame was once again burning brightly.

"Tell him it's been a success," she said. "He's not very far away from you."

That night I declaimed the fact to the sea and the stars, and hoped he was tuned in. In fact, I had not sensed a real closeness to him for some time, and certainly not while in the company of others. There is simply too much noise in your head when you are having to give attention to other people to be able to sense it. But neither does it come only in moments of quiet, as you might expect. Nor is there any point in struggling to hear it. It can come at any time, bursting through with an intensity that cannot be ignored, so you must be patient. But the mind needs to be in a certain, undefinable frame. That's the tricky bit. You can't plan for it. You must simply be ready to accept it when it arrives, and recognise it as something different from the ordinary. You must also be resigned to the thought that you might never hear it again. That is how it is.

I became aware of many kinds of perfections over this time, and of harmonies too. It does not take too much romantic imagination to find pleasure in the sea and stars — that's easy; but I started to appreciate for the first time the sheer beauty of the curve of the sails as they captured the wind and drove us forward. It seemed the most perfect thing in the world, how they achieved a balance and a harmony with the wind. When the wind, sea, wave and ship are working as one, then it is as close to a perfect motion as you can imagine. But the paradox of perfection is that it requires to stand alongside imperfection or it has no meaning, and boats

247

and the sea can be relied upon to provide plenty of that.

A deluge of rain, of the proportions that only the tropics can provide, caused the little anchor light to drown and my nights were completely black now. I could only trust to luck that someone else was not depending on that light in order to see and avoid me. This was a reasonable risk as we were well off the shipping lanes and way too far offshore for fishing boats to be a problem. Inshore, it would have been a different matter. I was now north of Rio, which gave me great heart, and a text message from Malcolme, now several weeks back home, reminded me that "it will soon be over, you know." There seemed far too much distance stretching ahead for this ever to be the case; too many thousands of miles to sail, too many waves to cross. But he was right, and I resolved to try and find pleasure in any aspect, no matter how small, knowing that the experience was already slipping from my grasp as the miles went by.

Such noble intent did not last long and waves of temper soon roared around the boat. I was expecting easterly winds now and the damned things didn't come. I kicked things, flung fists into the chart table, shouted at the poor boat, but no breeze blew. Then, out of the blue, the ripples on the water came from a new direction and I thought my troubles were over. But I was being made a fool of. It was the early signs of a rain squall, which, as I had learned over many thousands of miles, takes you in every direction but always leaves you more or less where you started. I had found myself in a battleground between two weather systems — the south-east trades were wanting to nudge in, as they eventually must, but the northerlies born of the south Atlantic High were not quite ready to give way. There was stalemate as they struggled for supremacy.

Nevertheless, anxious to ring up the curtain on another act, I tacked and tacked all night, often pointlessly, until miracle of miracles the wind settled into the east. Not for a minute, or an hour, but for a whole day, and for another after that. Not strong, but sufficient to give us decent progress, although given the strength of the wind and our speed through the water, I guessed that some tropical vegetation had found a home on the underwater section of the hull and was slowing us down. It felt a real drag.

I settled into my new-found weather system, which gave comfortable sailing. I felt the bit between my teeth now and made all haste towards to the equator some 900 miles distant. It was time to get worried about something else. I fretted for a whole day about whether or not I would have sufficient gas to last me the trip. The thought of no hot food or drink filled me with horror. Several pages of fine calculations were made and the judgement arrived at that if the present propane bottle lasted for another seven days (when I would be almost halfway to the Azores), then I had no worries. Even so, I put everything on ration and did not waste so much as a therm; I filled the kettle from a mug so as to boil only the amount of water necessary. Life became frugal.

Progress meant many small changes, not least that my beloved Southern Cross was rising lower in the sky every dusk, and the sun that had been passing to our north at midday would soon be overhead at noon before passing to the south of us. The sun and I were on the same journey for it too was travelling north to bring summer to the folks back home. Heavy rain showers came through at about five o'clock each night and I remember these as being the afternoon downpours so frequently felt in Salvador — we were on roughly the same latitude.

Any kind of failure in any of the boat's systems breeds unease. It might be no more than a couple of undone stitches in the sailcloth, or the end of rope that has become unravelled, but taken together they are a sharp reminder of your vulnerability. For that reason, I tried to fix everything that showed the slightest signs of weakness. But the computer I could not fix. It was not vital in the sense that it was keeping me afloat, or even safe, but it was doing good service in allowing me a daily glimpse of the wind patterns up to five days ahead. It has been the dream of all navigators to be able to see into the meteorological future, and now that precious gift was mine through the GRIB files, easily downloaded but via an achingly slow satellite phone. The computer is needed to decode and display the resulting information on a map. But the computer screen showed only an outline of an apple, the sign of temptation. I tried all manner of keystrokes, and even violence, but only succeeded in doubling the sweat dripping from my brow. That image of the apple, with one bite taken, remained. Was it not from this that all of the sins of the world followed? Whatever, my sin had been to grow too dependent on it and I must now pay the price. Malcolme offered to text me his interpretations of the weather set-up, and I was grateful, but it was not the same as making your own judgements with the data before your own eyes. It felt too much like being under air traffic control, while at the same time I was grateful for his efforts.

Two hundred miles short of the equator I thought I might finally go mad. The wind died to nothing in a place where the south-east trade wind was supposed to blow. It was a mean trick. To add to it, I was clouted hard on the head by the slatting boom as the boat rocked wildly, the motion made even worse by the lack of wind. I was raising and lowering sails all day but it was futile. The boat would not move. Using the engine was an option, but not for long. The diesel was strictly limited and the next opportunity for replenishment over 2,000 miles away. At the very most I dared motor for 400 miles, but no further.

I could not understand why the wind was not blowing. We were well within the trade-wind belt and so I came to the conclusion — an entirely false one, as it turned out — that the doldrums had migrated southwards to spite me. So, what to do? I tried losing my temper again, thumping the damned computer, throwing punches at everything that got in my way and firing off torrents of verbal abuse into the air. If I did my fuel calculations once I did them a dozen times; trying to work out how far I could go, how much I dared risk using up the diesel, the dangers of running out. It was all too depressing, frustrating and anger-inducing. I knew I could get the boat to sail and make progress if the wind blew at least at 5 measly knots from any damned direction, but the needle hovered at a stubborn 3.9. I fired up. The sound of the engine drummed through my head till it almost split. Again I shouted at everything in an uncontrolled rage but nothing seemed to be listening. These are the times when you realise you are truly alone.

It was the worst day of the whole voyage, and the equator was still 200 miles from my grasp. It was a Wednesday and I had set myself the entirely artificial and unnecessary goal of getting across the line by Sunday. That was beginning to look like an ambition too far. I knocked back the revs till she was going hardly faster than tick-over to try to reduce the fuel consumption, and settled down for another night made even steamier by the heat rising from the engine. I remembered that a spare anchor light lurked somewhere and I emptied locker after locker till I found that, and rigged it from the backstay as dusk was falling. As I was doing so, I became aware of two black shapes hovering in the sky. Two birds — clearly not seabirds for they had nothing of a gull about them — came to play around the rays of light. One landed on the metal frame of the spray hood. He had a long, curved, black beak, a white head, and a steely look in his eye that told me he had taken up residence and was not to be messed with. I approached him, possibly as close as six inches, but he didn't make a move, so filled with self-confidence was he. He shuffled himself a little until he was comfortable again and then stared blankly ahead, as if on watch.

But he was not just keeping lookout, for when I looked forward it became clear he was communicating with his friends who were gathering at the bow. There were four of them, identical black shapes in the gathering night. Where were they from? Brazil was several hundred miles to the west, Africa an even greater distance to the east. They had travelled some miles before landing on my little ship and as they glanced at me, then upwards at my limp sails, I wondered if it was crossing their minds how pathetic my wings were compared to theirs. I feared that like so many migrating birds they had dropped in, exhausted, seeking a place on which to die. By the morning, though, they were gone.

A cheery text message from Malcolme, now my chief weather adviser, told me there was no wind for another 300 miles. He was wrong. There was wind, and it came lightly from the south-east. This was the worst possible news.

CHAPTER
NINETEEN

REACHING OUT FOR
THE EQUATOR

I was sailing slowly into a black hole of my own making, although I did not know it at the time. I was much later to discover my speculation that the doldrums had moved southwards had been as fanciful as a chocolate teapot. It had not been the doldrums through which I had been struggling at all, it had been an unusual chasm in the south-east trade winds. The real doldrums still lay many hundreds of miles ahead.

I spent a long night chasing squalls in return for little real progress. Some brought heavy downpours of rain and I charged around trying to rig my home-made rain catcher, which I tied to the end of the boom, hoping to capture the water that ran in sheets down the mainsail. During one spectacular deluge I became so thrilled at the sight of my water can filling that I forgot to close the window above the chart table and went below to find everything awash. I grabbed the vital and only chart of the entire south Atlantic Ocean, but it fell apart at the fold as I tried to lift it. With luck, it was the western part that had turned to pulp and the section I was using I managed to salvage by careful drying.

A grey day brought with it long sinister swells with peaks and troughs like a Dales landscape, but no wind. Any breeze that lasted more than half an hour was considered a gift of God. I grew to hate the sound of the mainsail empty of wind; like a stomach, it grumbles if not full and I shared its hunger for progress. I risked motoring for another night with my fuel reserves ever dwindling. The equator seemed always more distant than my furthest grasp.

Still thinking the doldrums had migrated south and I was stuck in them, I imagined the sky ahead beginning to look less doldrum-like and the trade winds to be not far away. But no north-east wind ever blew. I eventually crossed the equator in the early evening of March the 25th at 2053 UTC and in my relief almost forgot my tribute to King Neptune. I went to the drinks locker and flung him a meagre thimbleful of spirit. It was done more out of duty than as a gesture of thanks, for it soon dawned on me that very little had happened. His majesty had bestowed on me no favours that day. Still, I was back in the northern hemisphere so I was home in that sense, but nothing had really changed.

With only one day's worth of fuel left, I motored on. Time became as artificial a construct as this imaginary line I had just crossed. Way back, I used to wake in the morning and wonder how I would pass all the hours of the day, but now the time just seemed to ebb past me like a stream washes over a rock. I didn't have to do anything, or make any effort; it just went by, ignoring me. I read Hemingway's *The Old Man and the Sea* and

255

noted the similarity between his futile efforts and mine. What were we both really trying to reel in?

And then came a blessed moment. Like all changes in the weather it arrives not with a fanfare but a whisper. The sun was setting and I was gathering my mental strength for yet another night played out to the disturbing beat of the engine. Then, on the surface of the ever-blackening sea, I saw a distinct ripple — the first sign of a breeze after calm. Those ripples were coming straight out of the north-east, just as nature intended: a harbinger, surely, of the longed-for north-east trade winds. I did not dare to think they were real, and tried to ignore them, certain they would go away. I was fully prepared for them to disappear, or change direction. I had spent so long hoping for this moment that I was more than ready to accept it as no more tangible than wishful thinking. That teasing ripple persisted though, just visible on the surface of the sea even if unfelt on my face. The mainsail slatted and in a gesture of defiance at the portent of wind, I ignored it and dropped the sail. I wasn't going to fall for its tricks again. I went below.

Within half an hour I was back on deck; the strengthening breeze could no longer be ignored. I re-hoisted the main, set the jibs, cut the engine, and set a course into the face of the darling north-east trade winds. How I loved them, to start with.

I had expected them to blow around force four, as the pilot books promised for this time of year, but they came in at a healthy force six and with more north in them than I wished. Things are never quite right. The best course I could lay had me pointing well towards New York. At every turn, the Atlantic Ocean seemed to have done its best to keep me away from home. I bashed off a bad-tempered email to Libby who told me, by swift return, that many others had managed what I am trying to do, and so would I eventually. She was right, of course. You cannot pray for wind and then moan when you get some.

I had become adept at baking bread, but claim no real skills, for in the tropical warmth dough rises like a rocket and within an hour of mixing it was billowing from the tin like a fluffy pillow. The bread was a great comfort, and when I had convinced myself that we were not going to run out of gas I made free with toast and eventually baked a weekly cake, although I did not have any sugar and instead used honey, which gave the resulting slab the texture of a scone rather than an intended Victoria sponge. No matter, with plenty of jam it lifted the spirits, and afternoon tea and cake became a fixture in the day. We bashed on, green water across the decks most of the time. I still had 400 miles to sail till I was abreast of the Cape Verde islands, where the north-east wind could be expected to moderate. It turned into a long, wet thrash in some of the biggest seas of the entire trip. Every jolt as the boat hit an oncoming wave and every crack as she fell into a trough added to my sense that the boat was becoming as tired as I was. Breakages might soon start to appear. Trade winds are best, I decided, when they are blowing from behind you.

The north-east trade winds persisted, stubbornly, from the north and I was driven further west towards America and away from home. To be as shaken and stirred as I was by the ever-growing seas was frustrating enough, but to be making little progress towards home led to yet another day of shouting at inanimate charts and instruments. It was boat abuse, plain and simple, and futile. My left eye became troublesome and I bathed it in eyewash three or four times a day, but it ached, as did most of me.

With the latitude of the Cape Verde islands still to be achieved, I started to tune the shortwave radio to weather transmissions broadcast from England by the Royal Navy in the form of fax charts. These are received as a series of warbling sounds, ten minutes of them to each chart with a rhythm of clicks and bleeps which, when decoded by a computer (or iPad in my case), give you a synoptic chart of the whole Atlantic Ocean, not just for the day but for five days ahead. These were like gold dust; now I was able to get the strategic overview that Malcolme's short text messages were not able to supply. The charts showed several days to come of plugging into these winds and seas, so were hardly cheering. On deck, frustration crept in as the wind piped up to 25 knots, dropped to 15, then went back up to 30 in a five-minute cycle, leading to slopping and crashing in cross seas that threw the boat in all directions.

There is little to do other than take to your bunk, although rest does not come easy. A fantasy life starts to take over, hallucinations perhaps. I invented an entire new life for myself ashore, with people I hardly knew, and had real conversations with them. They were my new world. I had had enough of the one I was in, and the one where I truly belonged was out of my grasp. I had to settle instead for a world of my own invention. So strong were these images that when I woke in the morning I expected to see my new friends there, and I would start conversations about the things we had discussed in my dreams.

A change in the sea always brings a change in frame of mind. I remember the evening the north-east trade winds finally ceased their blow. It was the 13th of April at 25 degrees north. I felt a deep sense of relaxation that night, as if a peak had finally been scaled. For the first time in weeks the boat was sailing upright across an undisturbed sea, wafting along in a failing breeze. Every sound, every rattle, every creak, became clear and distinct, almost painful to the ears, in a way I had forgotten. I enjoyed the evening warmth for a little while and went below, clapped earphones around my head and lapped up the sounds of piano.

After a while, when the music stopped, I removed the headphones and slowly my ears adjusted to the sound of water chuckling along the side of the hull. It was a sound so sweet and so intense that I thought, at the time, it was the most beautiful thing I had ever heard. Slowly other sounds came into focus: the swish of the water in the kettle, the tapping of the swaying coffee jar, the creak of the mainsheet against its winch. The silence at the song's end had brought me back to my real world, but one of greater clarity and intensity. The piano music had itself been intense, but the return to the real world was more sharply focused by it. The silence at the song's end was a world, but a better one.

That thought had hardly come into my mind when I felt an unusual motion of the boat, unlike any I had felt before. It came from the stern, as if someone or something was giving her a kindly push on her way.

From that moment on, the skies and seas became bluer and the air cleared of tropical moisture to leave arresting cloud formations, the changing shapes of which could be enjoyed just as much as if watching a movie. The days were cooler and at times the evenings felt chilly, and flocks of birds — migrating, I assumed — flew northwards, high overhead. Progress became slow again, but not frustrating. I decided that it is a godly kind of hand that takes little ships across the seas, and sometimes the hand is rough and you brace yourself for a struggle, but when the hand is soft and gentle then the sensation is peaceful beyond imagining.

I focused on an imaginary "1,000 miles to the Azores" barrier and started to believe that once I had cracked that it would be all downhill from there. That barrier was hell to break in persistent light winds, but I was cheered to find dolphins alongside, which I identified as the Atlantic spotted dolphin. They kept me good company for almost a day and we chatted. I thought about trailing a fishing line but was overcome with guilt at the thought of an assault on a fellow traveller. I even found myself scanning the horizon for white-capped waves. Can you believe that? It seemed

260

hardly more than a few days since I had bid them farewell, glad to see the back of them. Some days I just gave up trying to make progress. Then I lost my best winch handle over the side, which didn't please me, so I went below to bake the weekly cake.

I had been reading Nicholas's book quite intensely around this time, and so much of his character is recreated by his prose that it was difficult to believe he was not sailing with me. I could drop the book, turn my head, and see him sitting in the corner of the cabin just beyond the swinging oil lamp. In a gentle way, he would be telling me I was doing well. He always had a kind thought, rarely a sour one, and always showed genuine concern for how I was feeling. We never had a row that I can remember, perhaps because I understood him so well. He had too much of me in him for me not to understand what might be going through his mind. I knew too how easily he could be hurt, as can I.

I would love him to know I had made this trip, and grasped the adventure as nervously but determinedly as he took hold of his. That night, I saw in the sky the whole of the Plough for the first time, leading me home.

The Horse Latitudes are hateful and I am left in no doubt as to why the poor horses loathed them so much. The wind was light, the course was poor, the speed was down, the diesel was draining away, the food was getting boring and the sun was too damned hot again. How sick I had become of it all. As a diversion, the florescent light in the galley burst into flames that night and filled the boat with the stench of burning plastic.

The warbling fax messages made a return after a blank spot of a few hundred miles when reception was so bad that nothing could be decoded from the atmospheric hash. I had only 200 miles to go to the Azores but progress had again come to a halt for reasons that soon became clear as the fax images built across the screen. A large area of low pressure had, unusually, formed to the south of the Azores. As Malcolme cheerfully pointed out in one of his texts — to port were headwinds, to starboard fair winds, but where I was there was nothing at all and not likely to be for several days. Dark clouds passed overhead and torrential downpours followed in quick succession, drowning the wind instrument at the top of the mast, although I needed no electronics to tell me there was no wind at all. The sea got up, heaping itself into spiky clumps of water as if I had been caught in a tide race, but there was no breeze to stir it. I assumed some deep and sinister current was working its way to the surface and making itself felt.

To be disabled at the centre of a vast low pressure area is to understand that the word to describe this meteorological phenomenon — "depression" — was never more accurate. I suffered it for two days and early on the second the engine spluttered and gasped, fading, the life going from it, indicating that the last of the fuel was gone. That night, a feeble swallow landed on deck. Intent on Europe for the summer, as was I, it was clearly not going to make it. It was dead by morning. I would sail out of depression, for I knew that not far away the sun would be shining and the world would be a better place. But not everyone makes that leap of thought. For some, for one in particular, the notion of better things ahead was a belief too far.

I noted in the log on the following day that a gentle breeze had set in. Perfect, I described it. Damn this fickle place they call the sea.

I was just one hundred miles south of the Azores now. "Where's the damned westerlies?" I demanded of Malcolme, several times. He told me they were far to the north. Then came a message that began with the words, "Don't shoot the messenger but . . ."

Gale-force north-east winds were being shown, blowing with increasing strength straight from the direction I wished to go. I went to the chart and planned my strategy and tried to work out how far south-east I should sail before tacking, and how far to go before I could tack back and lay a course for Horta, my dreamed-of destination, only 150 miles away. The wind was slowly strengthening, the seas were already building, and *Wild Song* sailed further and further away from her course, rendering all my plans futile. It was going to be a long slog. The wind finally gathered its strength, as forecast, and made it to a full gale. I decided to heave-to. With over 15,000 miles under my belt I should have known that the dear boat had more in her than this, and to make progress in a gale was more than possible. I should have bashed on. But I was now the weak link in the chain. I had feared that it would be parts of her that would break, but now I thought it more likely that it would be me. I had had enough. I hove to at 38.34N 29.42W, a mere 53 miles south-west of Horta. In hindsight, I cannot believe I was so close, but my mind had been used to calculating in thousands of miles and I had lost any real sense of distance.

Hove to, the boat sat comfortably and I settled myself down for what I expected to be 24 hours of gale-force winds, followed by a moderation. The motion was easy. I was able to read and cook even as the seas built. Only the occasional wave crashed on board, but I was not concerned. But as the seas grew over time and darkness fell, I felt less secure. One tumbling wave washed over us so that the cabin windows were beneath green water. We were now submarining and cascades of cold seawater tumbled down the ventilators, flooding the galley and chart table. I opened a hatch in the cabin floor and saw that the bilge was brim full of water. The sea was rising in every direction and getting a little too close for comfort. I rigged the emergency pump and in 150 strokes had the bilge dry.

Then a wave, bigger than the rest and mischievous too, fell across us. The boat lurched and the thump of tons of water was such that it felt as though we had sailed straight into a concrete wall, with the crack so sharp and wilful that I could not believe the hull had not been split open like a cracked nut. I leapt to the hatch and looked out. The triple-reefed mainsail, sheeted hard amidships, was intact. So was everything else apart from a solar panel that had been ripped from its mount, and I was to get severely soaked while working on the aft deck to secure it. It was dusk and I had no intention of being up there longer than I needed and so quickly glanced around. Everything seemed fine, if soaked.

I had a nervous exchange of messages with Libby. How unfair to share your fears with someone ashore who can do nothing to help you. "Do you want rescuing?" she asked at one point. This brought me up sharp. Rescuing? Certainly not! Nonsense. As so many times before, a carefully chosen word from her brought me back to my senses.

The expectation was that the following morning the wind and sea would be down. From my bunk I could see the instruments and I must have woken every ten minutes in the night to see the needles still showing a strong gale blowing. By dawn, though, it had dropped to force seven and I knew I must try to make progress once again. It was now that I made a great mistake. I should have set my face to the wind and no matter how tough it might have been, I should have bashed away the remaining miles to Horta. It would have been rough and wet and horrible. I know now, although I did not at the time, that the boat would have made it. But I had been seduced by the island of Flores some 30 miles to my north-west. I had been watching the GPS overnight and, remarkably, it showed that my downwind drift set me directly on the island. Once I could sail again I could run off, tuck myself in the lee of the island, and find shelter in an anchorage the pilot book described as good shelter in strong easterly winds. I had no fuel, so no engine, but surely I could sail into shelter. Slightly more unnerving was the fact that I had no paper charts

265

and the electronic map on my plotter did not cover this region, but I was in a determined and stubborn frame of mind and decided I would overcome all these small irritations.

I set to making my own chart. The pilot book had sketch charts and the text confirmed that Flores had no dangers that were not visible. I could sail quite safely by just keeping my eyes open. As for the anchorage, I had its coordinates and so could use the GPS to find the spot.

Dawn broke. The sea looked vile and as rough as any I had ever sailed in before. My first job was to drop the main as I wanted to sail in with headsail alone. I thought through every move I would make, because to get a halyard tangled would add great complication in these big seas. I unlashed the helm and put it over, and as the bow paid off I gave her a scrap of jib. She bowled off, glad to be on the move again, making a nice 4 knots and 30 miles to go to the sound between Flores and the island of Corvo, a couple of miles to the north. How I cursed the wind direction. Flores has a perfectly good harbour, at Lajes, but its breakwater was wide open to the current wind and seeing the size of the swell I guessed it would be like a cauldron in there. That, it turned out, was one of my better judgements.

I was just 5 miles off yet neither of these two islands could be seen. The fog was down and I cursed it. Now and then I would get a glimpse of land to the south, then a flash of land ahead, and I even saw Corvo clear against the sky, but this northern tip of Flores remained under a shroud. I may have been no more than a mile off before I could make out land for absolute certain. I crept round the headland and soon expected to find shelter. Certainly the water looked flatter, calm almost, and I started to feel a great sense of relief as I hardened the sheets, having set a little mainsail and started to work my way down the island's west coast, tack after tack.

The first unexpected blast of wind hit with a force I could not have imagined. The gust came out of nowhere. At one moment we were in a calm, the next the needle was showing 40 knots. The boat heeled and laboured and I quickly reefed the jib till it was a mere scrap. Then the gust left us and we wallowed, making no progress. I let out more sail, only to be clouted round the head by the next blast. Since we had come to a halt between the gusts and had no forward speed, we were being pushed further and further out to sea and ever more distant from the anchorage. The pilot book had not warned of katabatic winds. I thought they were all 7,000 miles behind me.

Sailing becomes almost impossible when the wind switches from 35 knots to nothing every minute. I noticed a small, rocky outcrop to leeward (which I had expected) and made a course to clear it, losing even more distance. For some reason the boat seemed sluggish and reluctant to tack. She would come up into the wind, then stick there before falling back on the tack from which she had just come. At the wrong moment, such a move could have dangerous consequences and I could be driven on to rocks with no engine to save me.

The effort of tacking was taking its toll on my arms. In order to get her through the wind I needed good boat speed and to achieve that I needed plenty of sail. But that brought with it the effort of winding in the sail when full of wind, which had to be done with great speed or ground would be lost. I could not miss a beat.

On occasions she would not tack at all, so to get her round I had to "wear", or gybe, the boat. Instead of tacking through the wind you put her stern through it — as the old, unhandy sailing ships used to do. I did this several times and lost ground every time. Then, just as I was gybing once again, we were hit by a squall I did not see coming and as the boom slammed across, the mainsail ripped along its full length and hung in tatters — it is known as a Chinese gybe. I looked up at the ripped sail in complete shock, yet somehow pulled myself together sufficiently to haul it down and bundle it up. As I was doing this, I caught out of the corner of my eye a grey shape in the water. A dolphin? No, it was the damned grey inflatable dinghy, which had been washed overboard the night before and which I had been towing underwater for 30 miles, completely unaware it was there. This, I now realised, was the cause of the sluggishness. I cut the old friend adrift with a heavy heart for she had felt like a part of the family. I dare say she is still out there, bobbing along, if not in America by now.

With no mainsail, no engine, and in such variable wind ranging from calm to gale force, it was going to be a struggle to make the anchorage, but I was determined that I would not drift out into the Atlantic, next stop

268

Bermuda. I set a jib and a little staysail and tried to sail in, but we wallowed in the calms and the head was blown off when the wind returned, so what little ground had been gained was again lost. I'd eaten no food for twelve hours, so I stabbed the autopilot button, although I wasn't certain that the batteries carried enough reserve to run it. All I needed was time to make tea. I felt close to passing out.

I tacked and tacked again until my arms turned to jelly. I could see the anchorage, the pier, the village, but I could not get into the calmer waters inshore. Every tack felt like reaching with an outstretched arm for the shore, but it remained just beyond the tips of my fingers. Without her mainsail to drive her, the boat struggled. "Tack for Daddy, tack for Daddy," I urged her.

I sensed darkness falling. I had been tacking, pointlessly, for over five hours, winding in the sail, hardly able to catch my breath before it was time to tack and wind it in again. I glanced up at the mast and saw everything up there was now in a tangle. I made one last tack. This one would have to do. But as I let the sheet fly and went forward to let go the anchor, I found the chain had jammed and the anchor would not run free. By now we were out of shelter again and the tacking recommenced. I had nothing left in me. The shore lights were coming on. I made one last tack inshore, let fly, dashed forward, and this time the anchor rattled to the seabed. I let go all 60 metres of chain in 15 metres of water. When the anchor bit, the boat lurched to a standstill with such force that I was almost off my feet, but at least I knew it had bitten. We were going no further that night. It was not the stylish arrival I had planned.

I dived for the winch to reef the flapping headsail, mindful that this was my last working sail. The reefing was jammed. I unlatched the halyard and thought of dropping the sail on to the deck, but that was jammed too. I have no idea how I stilled that sail, I have no memory of what I did or what I used, but somehow its flapping was eventually silenced. It was now completely dark.

I assessed my position. The anchor was holding. Every few minutes I checked my position against a shore light. We did not budge an inch and I blessed the money I had spent on that galvanised iron brute of an anchor. The mainsail was shredded, the engine would not go, I had no diesel, the water was becoming short and the food had only a few days left. I was soaking wet and trembling from the exertion of previous hours. I felt, if not entirely safe, then in as good a position as I could have hoped to be in. For the moment, that would have to do.

CHAPTER
TWENTY

THE SONG'S END

I have never before asked for assistance and consider it a kind of failure. "Every herring should hang by its own tail" is my borrowed motto. This particular fish, though, was feeling a bit washed up. After so much gruelling winch-grinding, and the struggle to dowse the headsail, I had little of anything left in me — certainly no fight. I was too tired to eat, and rather than cook some much-needed food I chose instead to rip the lid off a tin of rice pudding and ate that, cold, directly from the tin. Many times I glanced out of the galley window, where I watched like a hawk a transit between a light on the shore and a stanchion on the boat. We were holding firm, so that was one concern less. Land looked so close but I knew it was still so far.

If I was to make it to Lajes, which was a mere 10 miles round the corner to the south, several things were going to have to happen and at that moment all of them seemed unlikely. I had expected to be anchored closer inshore and able to get to the village by the remaining spare dinghy, but from well out and almost in open water it was impossible, given the rough state of the sea. This meant I could not expect to get any diesel, without which the engine was not going to work. Without the engine, I was soon going to run out of electricity after several overcast days had rendered the solar panels of little use. Without electricity it would be a struggle to raise the anchor and the torn muscles in my arms did not relish the prospect of getting it up by hand, which in any wind would be nigh on impossible anyway. More importantly, the weather would have to change for me to be able to do anything. But here was the paradox: for the harbour at Lajes to become tenable, the wind would have to drop or move from the north-east. If it were to become westerly, though, I would find myself on a lee shore and in an even worse position. Other than going calm, which was unlikely, however the weather changed it would leave me in a worse position than the one I was already in. If all else failed I suppose I could have cut and run from here out into the Atlantic, but in a westerly wind I might have the same struggle to get out as I had to get in. I noticed my phone had come to life so I called Falmouth Coastguard in the UK and told them that I was in no distress, but needed assistance. The comfort of a calm and authoritative voice from home was welcome. With surgical efficiency, my position was noted and so was my request for a tow. Within ten minutes of ending the call, the phone rang again. It was the Azores Coastguard calling from their HQ. Yes, they could arrange a tow. Would I like it now or in the morning? Was I OK? I told them all was now well and with a further check of the transit between that lovely light on the shore and the stanchion on the boat, I turned in.

It was a shallow sleep from which I woke at dawn to find no change in the weather. The sea was still rough, the wind was still blowing. I had one slice of bread left and toasted that and topped it with a tin of tomatoes as I sat and waited for my rescuers. Let them come soon. I had no idea what to expect. My fear was that a rather feeble little fishing boat would appear and the skipper would then shake his head sadly at the enormity of the task before leaving me to my fate. The manager of the marina called about nine to tell me a boat was on its way. This was good news. But by twelve it hadn't appeared and again I feared the worst.

In the end the very best happened and a powerful take-it-on-the-chin kind of pilot launch appeared with a crew of four strong lads who landed on the deck with a thump and a look on their faces that said they were ready for action. I noticed they had no protective clothing, no life jackets, none of the kit that we are used to seeing draped around our own rescue services, but they had an enthusiasm about them evident from the broad grins on their faces. It could have been another dreary day of harbour work for them, but here was some diverting action.

I could never have managed without them. I had thought that if I could buy diesel I would be able to get the engine going, but I later discovered that it needed the magic spanner of a local engineer to achieve its resurrection. It also took all four of these beefy blokes the best part of half an hour to raise all 60 metres of anchor chain, fighting every link of it as the force seven wind continued to blow. The skipper of the pilot launch steered with much skill and confidence, and on the four or five occasions on which the tow parted while perilously close to rocks, he slipped his boat into precisely the right position to prevent disaster.

After two hours we rounded the breakwater and headed for a narrow gap in a harbour wall with rocks on either side. This was the marina entrance, although with the swell that was running it might as well have been the gates of hell. It revealed itself as the most optimistic marina ever built, for it could offer little protection in any swell from the north-east; hardly surprising when you consider you are effectively tying up to a small rock in the middle of the Atlantic Ocean. Once inside, and after the tow line had been let go, I drove her towards a berth where people were waiting to grab my lines. With no engine all I could do was steer, and to bring the boat to a halt I had to rely on the solid pontoon to stop us. My long haul up the Atlantic Ocean came to an end with an earsplitting crunch.

Lajes was hardly a placid haven, and in the three days it took for the wind to moderate and the swell to die down, life on board often felt as wild as if I had still been at sea. A French yacht had found it all too much, made their boat secure, then headed for a hotel to try and get some sleep.

It had not been the tranquil reintroduction to shore life I had expected. I have often been asked if I had difficulty communicating with or meeting people, after so long alone. I had no such problems. Instead, I revelled in the joy of shopping, of getting the boat in order, of coming back down to earth. I bought eggs and bacon and ate them for nearly every meal, simply because I could. I loved the scents of the island: the smells of earth and flowers that were as rich and intense as that cloud of fragrance that assaults your entry to a department store. Everything felt simply beautiful. Birdsong had an intensity that I had never experienced before and I could sit for hours, transfixed by it. Food was limited in the way that all island supplies are, but the joy of choice, any old choice, more than made up for it. Just up the hill from the harbour was a small cafe with a bar. It had a television blaring football and a few tables. As I walked in, a chap opened his arms and embraced me. "We have heard about you," he said. "You are the old-timer!" It was meant as a compliment. I asked if there was food? "Pizza tonight," the woman said. I wasn't certain about pizza, and she sensed it from the look on my face. "OK then, it's meat tonight," she offered. A young Belgian sailed in a few days later, fresh from his solo crossing from Guadeloupe in a 19-foot boat he had built himself from sheets of plywood — "It goes really well in a gale." Below, his tiny craft looked like the scene of a natural disaster. "But I've already tidied up," he asserted. He worked on gas tankers as an engineer, deep in the engine room for twelve-hour shifts with no sight of daylight or sea. I asked him why he'd made the solo trip. "So I can look my bloody skipper in the eye and say to him, 'I've sailed the Atlantic Ocean alone, and you haven't. So fuck you!'" He was quite right. To be able to make such as claim, if used sparingly, is often a comfortable position in which to find yourself.

I was on the island of Flores a full week. At times, though, getting jobs done was like a long trek through treacle. Some places are just too relaxed about life. I waited first for a man to get the engine going, but there was a public holiday and he was delayed. Then I waited for someone to climb the mast to unwrap all manner of bits of string that had flayed around and become tangled. Then I waited for the truck that brought the diesel. Most importantly I was waiting for the wind to drop, for I had no intention of making a rough sail of it to Horta, 120 miles away, mindful that I still had no mainsail. I waited till the sea was flat calm and crept out, engine now running sweetly. I unrolled the headsail and saw that some of stitching looked feeble, with daylight visible through small rips. The sails were in a truly sorry state. I was all too aware that we were limping along. For every single one of those miles from Flores to Horta I prayed the engine to maintain its rattling and thumping. I held my breath at every subtle change in its note. Had it failed, I would have got there somehow or other, but I don't know how. Twenty-four hours after leaving I was having my passport stamped in Horta, and I moored beneath a shop selling exquisite coffee in a harbour with luxurious showers and a laundry. Horta felt like heaven and the sounds of Duncan Sweet's voice as calming as that of an angel.

Duncan and his wife have a shop they call "The Biggest Little Chandlery in the World". It was truly tiny compared to some, but everything was to be found here and Aladdin would have felt at home. Whatever I asked for, they had, somewhere. The greatest thing, though, was the size of the hearts of these two people, who were non-stop in their support. She told me, cautiously, that she had heard the radio play assembled by Libby from Nicholas's writings. It had made a deep impression on her so it gave me more than pleasure to give her a copy of his book, for I had carried several on board. I thought how comforting to find his flame burning in the most unlikely places.

I took a refreshing hotel room for a couple of nights and could have stayed on that island (this "damned lovely lump of rock" as Duncan referred to it) for ever, but it was time to be heading home, which was now only 1,200 miles away. The weather had not changed its mood but had merely taken a pause from its incessant blowing from the north-east, the direction of home. I made friends with a neighbouring boat, also homeward bound for Devon. There was much shaking of heads at the thought of gales, now blowing a few hundred miles to the north. This was too unfair. But we both set off, as we knew we must eventually, and I suffered a sharp reminder that not only was I tired but the boat was too, when the stainless-steel tube from which hangs the self-steering paddle cracked, leaving the paddle trailing behind. It had had enough and snapped. I felt pretty much the same. At least I got a night at anchor off San Jorge while I fixed it and enjoyed a full night's sleep I wasn't expecting.

I have been putting off my final thoughts about Nicholas's poem, the inspiration for this voyage. I feared they may sound silly, or sentimental. I have to accept that. But I have pondered his words on and off for over nearly 18,000 miles and whichever way my thoughts have taken me they have come back to the same place.

> *I sing, as I was told,*
> *inside myself.*

> *I sing inside myself*
> *the one wild song, song that whirls*
> *my words around*
> *until a world unfurls*

> *my ship's new sail*
> *I catch the dew and set*
> *a course amongst the ocean curls*

> *The silence at the song's end*
> *Before the next*
> *Is the world.*

I asked myself first what was the song that he was told to sing, and by whom? And what might that internal music be that drives his ship?

There is a song within us all. I know this now because in the long silences of the open ocean I have heard it. It resounds. It is perpetual. It cannot be ignored. It is sweet. You can try to dismiss it, but it is more forceful than you are; it can drive you in ways of which you will not be conscious, for it is setting the tempo of your life even more strongly than the beat of your heart. Over time its volume will vary: one minute shrill, whispering the next. Yet it remains and is all-powerful.

I have always felt that there is some force within that drives me, keeps me pressing on no matter how strong the urges to falter might be. But it gives not only impetus; it defines me, and all of us, and makes us what we are, and without it we are nothing. You might call this music the voice of our souls.

There have been so many moments on this voyage when I could have turned tail, taken the easy option, settled for something less than the biggest prize, but I sailed on. I never really felt there was any other choice, not for long anyway. This is the power of the music inside and from it flows an unmatchable glow of reward for the achievements that determination delivers. That moment is the song's crescendo.

But who dictates the nature of our souls? By whom is the song taught or told? This is the most difficult of questions to answer and mine can only be a guess, but for me it must be God. That is what I have concluded Nicholas believed. And if it is true that God is the composer of this music, then that music can only be one thing — and it is the very sound of love. For love drives everything. It seems so crystal clear to me now. There is no greater driving force in the world. It was for love of Nicholas that I was driven to find a meaning in his words; it was love of the sea and sailing that drove my voyage. Love propelled me the length of the Atlantic Ocean, not wind or waves.

Science cannot define love, philosophy largely ignores it, our senses cannot detect it, yet it remains. You can, however, feel it and few would deny that. When, on those occasions I have felt Nicholas close to me on this voyage and heard a few of his words in my head, they were part of the song too, the song of love.

It was Nicholas's own song, inspired by his love of the sea and his ship that caused the song inside him to "*unfurl(s) my ship's new sail*," and to draw him into another world.

Yet what happens when the song ends, when the silence comes? I mentioned in passing a night a thousand miles back when my headphones were clamped to my head and the uplifting sounds of piano music were pumping across my brain. Then the music ended, and faded to nothing. It was the song's end. Then the real world returned as its sounds crept round the headphones, and it came with a vengeance; the sounds of the sea and the boat became ever more intense and I saw the world around me with new clarity. The world was made more coherent and intense not just because of the song itself, but through the song ending. As perhaps life falls into complete clarity when it also ends.

But what would happen if the song ended and no world worth living in replaced it? What if the song's end did not lead to intensity, but to nothing?

I now think that is exactly the place where my poor boy ended up the night he died. The song ended, but no vision of a better place could his troubled mind discern. So everything ended.

280

★ ★ ★

Was the weather ever going to give me a break? I didn't ask a lot: just a few days of light, easy sailing with the sun on my back so I could arrive home with a smile on my face and a healthy rather than a haggard look. The weather systems that had given Europe a bitter winter prevailed even though it was now mid-May, and I was faced with incessant headwinds all the way home. I nursed the boat rather than driving her. Everything was damp or soggy despite a good drying out in the Azores. The lines looked ready to part, the sails ever more feeble. Even at this late stage I had no certainty I would make it.

Nor could I grapple with the reduced scale of what lay ahead. Everything up to now had been played out on a broad canvas where distances were measured in thousands, and now I was finding myself increasingly confined by a continent. Off Ushant, which Libby and I had rounded two years before, the wind freshened to a full gale from the north-west and the last hundred miles home seemed the longest of the trip so far. I was unused to the throng of big ships that were making their way up and down the English Channel, forcing me to play cat and mouse with each one of them. There was little chance for rest. As usual, I started too early with my calculations of my arrival time and one minute I was flashing Libby a message saying I would be in on Friday, then make that Saturday. No, I've been headed! Make that Sunday.

On the Friday night, my last night out, the sea in mid-Channel heaped up in a way I had not seen since

281

the Roaring Forties. Even though the weather charts promised an early moderation I had little trust any more. How could this gale blow itself out so quickly as to leave the windless conditions the forecast promised? But I should have kept the faith, for by mid-morning the gale had melted away as fast as an ice cream on a hot pavement and with just 30 miles to go I was left without a breath of wind.

I engaged forward gear, then the autopilot, and went to smother the sails for the last time. As I made my way to the foredeck I glanced up and saw land ahead. Not any old land but a pair of headlands I knew only too well — Start Point and Bolt Head, the southernmost extremities of Devon. I greeted them like a pair of old friends. It was not long before my old mate, the lighthouse itself on Start Point, could be made out, and with a few hours remaining of this voyage I set to making the weary old boat as spotless as I could.

It was about this time that the GPS clicked through the 18,000-mile mark. *Wild Song* had done me proud. Her sails were exhausted, rust streaks had formed on her hull where rust had no right to be. Everything above deck was crusted in salt as sea evaporated in the warm sun, leaving its chloride residue. The varnish was peeling, as I might if left out in the sun too long.

A final race was on now. I was heading north to Dartmouth, and Libby and daughter Rose were dashing down the M5 for a reunion, fighting an adverse tide of caravans at every one of Devon's roundabouts. Then, just after five in the afternoon, I was helped alongside by the harbour launch and not ten minutes later Libby and Rose appeared courtesy of the water taxi and we had our long-anticipated reunion, culminating in glorious hugs and a memorable fish and chip supper.

You might expect that such an adventure should end on a higher note, but you don't find soldiers cheering much when the battle is won. They prefer quiet satisfaction and the comforting thought that they have got away with it.

And that was how I felt as I remembered again the wise words of the old ocean adventurer who welcomed me to America after my solo Atlantic passage a decade ago. He said, "You won't think much of it now, but it will grow on you."

Or put it another way. The song inside me had been playing so loudly and with such intensity for the last two years that nothing could be heard above its din and nothing could eclipse it. It would take time to fade away, and only then would I be able to get a real perspective on this adventure.

I cannot forget, though, that there was one who voyaged with me for every mile that I sailed, and for whom the silence came and no world followed. He was not waiting for me in the harbour, not there to give and receive the hugs, not there to joke and laugh with.

Throughout this trip I knew he wasn't there, wasn't in the cabin, wasn't at the wheel, but that is not to say that he was nowhere. He is out there somewhere, I know, amongst his ocean curls. And for a brief while I was able to be with him.

And will be again when all our voyages become one.

BIBLIOGRAPHY

Patagonia and Tierra Del Fuego Nautical Guide, Mariolina Rolfo and Giorgio Ardrizzi, Editrice Incontri Nautici, 2nd edition 2007

Chile, Andrew O' Grady and others, Royal Cruising Club Pilotage Foundation 2004

Atlantic Islands, Anne Hammick, Royal Cruising Club Pilotage Foundation 2008

Brazil Cruising Guide, Michael Balette, Imray, 2nd edition 2010

Cape Horn, A Maritime History, Robin Knox-Johnston, Hodder and Stoughton 1995

Tierra del Fuego, R. Natalie P. Goodall (privately published in Ushuaia in English and Spanish) 1979

Rounding the Horn, Dallas Murphy, Basic Books, New York 2004

Patagonia A Cultural History, Chris Moss, Signal Books, Oxford 2008

Voyage of the Beagle, Charles Darwin, Penguin Classics 1989

Uttermost Part of the Earth, E. Lucas Bridges, The Rookery Press, New York 2007

Through the Land of Fire, Ben Pester, Seafarer Books 2004

ACKNOWLEDGEMENTS

Even though a large proportion of the voyage described in this book was conducted alone, that does not mean all the effort in achieving it was just mine.

I must thank my crews who came with me for the coastal legs. Chris Hamblin and Ant Bowring took the warm-water option and sailed as far as the Canaries.

Mike Purves and Alasdair Scott joined in Salvador and sailed to Rio and were rewarded with the attentions of the Rio muggers.

Chris Eakin joined in Uruguay and braved the Roaring Forties to get to Ushuaia. I am grateful to him for his photographs, and for putting me right on a few points concerning wine.

Mike Godfrey and Malcolme Collins bravely joined after only a brief meeting, and their trust was rewarded with a trip round the Horn. Malcolme distinguished himself when it came to preparing a cooked breakfast from sparse ingredients in the wildest of conditions, for which we are all grateful.

The hardest job lands on those who are left behind; in my case, Libby, my wife, and Rose, our daughter. They were unfailing in their messages of support when things were not going well, and without that encouragement I could not have made this trip. I apologise if any of my messages home were less than upbeat.

Of those I met along the way, I was grateful for the friendship of Sandoval at Pier Salvador; for the work done on *Wild Song* by Laurence Hildersley and his partner Elisa in Piriapolis; and to Roxanna Diaz for her logistical support in Ushuaia. In Puerto Williams, Chile, I thank the staff of *Micalvi* for their welcome, and Denis Chevallay for his caretaking of the boat while I was away. And thanks to Atilio Mosco whose steel ketch, *Ksar*, got me back to Ushuaia in time to catch my plane.

HM Coastguard in Falmouth were impressively efficient when I called them from off the Azores, as were the Azorean coastguard and the skipper and crew of the pilot launch that came to my rescue.

In Horta, I greatly appreciated the welcome and support of Mid Atlantic Yacht Services, in particular the basket of fruit they gave me for the final leg home.

Other titles published by Ulverscroft:

THE HOUSE IS FULL OF YOGIS

Will Hodgkinson

Once upon a time in the 1980s, the Hodgkinsons were just like any other family. Nev, Liz, Tom and Will lived the suburban dream. That is, until a questionable buffet gave Nev a bout of food poisoning which brought about a revelation. Their lives would never be the same again. Out went drunken dinner parties; in came hordes of white-clad Yogis meditating in the living room. While Tom took it all in his stride, the arrival of the Brahma Kumaris threw Will into crisis. As if that weren't enough, he also fell hopelessly in love with his best friend's sister . . .

IN SEARCH OF MARY

Bee Rowlatt

Toddler in tow, Bee Rowlatt embarks upon an extraordinary journey in search of the life and legacy of the first celebrity feminist: Mary Wollstonecraft. From the wild coasts of Norway to a naked re-birthing in California, via the blood-soaked streets of revolutionary Paris, Bee learns what drove her hero on, and what's been won and lost over the centuries in the battle for equality. On this biographical treasure hunt she finds herself consulting a witch, a porn star, a quiet Norwegian archivist and the tenants of a blighted council estate in Leeds — getting much more than she bargained for. In her quest to find a new balance between careers and babies, Bee also discovers the importance of celebrating the radiant power of love in all our lives.

A WOVEN SILENCE

Felicity Hayes-McCoy

How do we know that what we remember is the truth? Inspired by the story of her relative Marion Stokes, one of three women who raised the tricolour over Enniscorthy in Easter Week 1916, Felicity Hayes-McCoy explores the consequences for all of us when memories are manipulated or obliterated, intentionally or by chance. In the power struggle after the Easter Rising, involving, among others, Michael Collins and Eamon de Valera, the ideals for which Marion and her companions fought were eroded. As she maps her own family stories onto the history of the state, Felicity's story moves from Washerwoman's Hill in Dublin, to London, and back again; spans two world wars, a revolution, a civil war and the development of a republic; and culminates in Ireland's 2015 same-sex marriage referendum.

CHRISTMAS AROUND THE VILLAGE GREEN

Dot May Dunn

Derbyshire, 1940s: Christmas is different for little Dot May Dunn and her fellow villagers these days. The paper garlands are red, white and blue, though Father Christmas still comes, carols are sung, and families are relieved to be together. As the seasons change and war still rages, Dot must adjust to holidays, village fetes and school life under its shadow. She understands very little of the terrible events in the adult world; but as the village comes face to face with their effects, the real impact bears heavily on this close-knit mining community.